I0459318

"This biblically grounded support group curriculum is a much-needed resource for parents who are walking through the unimaginable pain of child loss. With its thoughtful blend of Bible study, personal reflection, guided discussion, and prayer, it creates space for grieving parents to bring both their sorrow and their faith into honest conversation with God and with one another. The companion book, filled with stories from fellow bereaved parents, offers comfort and assurance that the griever is not alone and provides real-life testimony to God's sustaining presence in the darkest valleys. Whether used independently or together, the curriculum and book invite parents into a Christ-centered journey of lament, hope, and healing that can truly transform the grief experience.

—Brad and Jill Sullivan,
Co-Founders of the While We're Waiting ministry

Eternal Surrender

A JOURNEY FOR PARENTS
WHO HAVE LOST A CHILD

Mike and Connie Washburn

Copyright © 2025 Mike and Connie Washburn

ISBN: 979-8-9906208-9-6

All rights reserved. No part of this publication may be reproduced, distributed, or transmitted in any form or by any means, including photocopying, recording, or other electronic or mechanical methods, without the prior written permission of the publisher, except in the case of brief quotations embodied in critical reviews and certain other noncommercial uses permitted by copyright law. No part of this book may be used as data for 'training' any Large Language Model or as part of any machine learning or neural network architecture.

All scriptures from the HOLY BIBLE, NEW INTERNATIONAL VERSION®, NIV®. Copyright © 1973, 1978, 1984, 2011 by Biblica, Inc. Used with permission. All rights reserved worldwide.

"O Praise the Name (Anastasis)" by Hillsong Worship. Copyright 2015 by Hillsong Music Publishing. Written by Benjamin Hastings, Dean Ussher, and Marty Sampson. Rights administered in the US and Canada by Capitol CMG Publishing.

All photos courtesy of their respective owners.

Cover design by Shull Design.
Interior formatting by SpineAndSpark.

Published by Mission Increase Publishing.

Table of Contents

We are incredibly grateful to our editor, Amy Hossler, for her tireless work in refining the writings of all the parents who participated in this book. Amy's love for the Lord radiates through her patience, her compassion and her work. We are eternally grateful for you.

Mike and Connie

Foreword

From

Mike and Connie Washburn

As a couple who has experienced deep and life-altering loss, we understand the pain, the confusion, and the overwhelming emptiness that can flood your heart. It's a path no one ever chooses, yet so many are forced to walk. Through our own grief and the ministry God has entrusted to us, we have come to know this heartache intimately—and also, the profound faithfulness of a God who meets us in the depths of sorrow.

Eternal Surrender is not just a title; it's an act of worship. In this book, you'll find the stories of families who have walked through the darkness of loss and experienced God's sustaining presence as they persevered. These stories are a testament to the truth that even in our deepest grief, we can trust God. He does not abandon us in our sorrow; He carries us through it, leading us from the shadows into the light.

This book is for you, for those moments when you may wonder if God is still with you or if life will ever hold joy again. Through these powerful stories, we pray you will see God's faithfulness as it unfolds in the lives of others, and be encouraged to fight to live again. Each page is a reminder that even in our deepest pain, God is trustworthy. We hope you will find comfort in knowing you are not alone, and that, just as God has carried others through their darkest days, He will do the same for you.

From

Mike and Connie~

Isaiah 43:2-3a

When you pass through the waters, I will be with you and when you pass through the rivers, they will not sweep over you. When you walk through the fire, you will not be burned; the flames will not set you ablaze. For I am the Lord your God, the Holy One of Israel, your Savior.

Knowing that God is close brings comfort. But knowing He is near in the midst of a storm is everything. As a parent who has lost a child, there will be times when God doesn't feel close, and the weight of grief feels overwhelming. Yet, in those moments, His promises remain unwavering. The Sovereign God, who protects and strengthens us, is with us even in the harshest of storms. Sometimes, He calms the storm. Other times, He carries us through it. But no matter what, He brings peace to our hearts, even as the storm rages around us. In the midst of your pain, He is there, holding you, guiding you, and offering you the strength to face each new day. You are never alone.

Cruz

By Mckenzie Manley,
His Mother

God Will Meet You in Your Empty

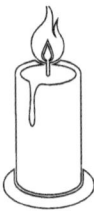

It was a picturesque autumn day, with the sun casting its warm glow and the fragrant essence of fall carried on a gentle breeze. One of the things I cherish about Nebraska is the opportunity to fully embrace all four seasons. While we savored the beauty of the day, I found myself engaged in conversation with my sister-in-law about a recent tragedy in our community. As we spoke, I said, "I can't even begin to imagine what it would be like to sit in the front row." Although I had attended funerals before, I had always been a part of the crowd, never occupying the space reserved for those closest to the one who had died. Witnessing the anguish etched on the faces of those in the front row as they entered the service was always heart-wrenching, but it was merely a glimpse of the profound grief they carried. While the rest of the congregation mourned, there was an undeniable weightiness to the front row—their sorrow ran deeper than I could comprehend. As we continued our conversation on that tranquil fall afternoon, the thought of the immense sorrow weighing on the family in the front row brought tears to my eyes. It felt unfathomable. Little did I realize that just a few weeks later, I would be confronting my own fear of occupying that very space.

Cruz Elias

Right from the start, our son Cruz made quite an entrance. After experiencing the heartbreak of a miscarriage during our first pregnancy, we were hesitant to embrace the idea of becoming pregnant again. Fears and doubts plagued our thoughts—what if history were to repeat itself? The magnitude of love we felt was shadowed by the fear of enduring another profound loss; the pain seemed unbearable. Yet, just two months later, we received the unexpected news of another pregnancy! In the midst of our storm, Cruz emerged as a beacon of light. We were so grateful for a healthy pregnancy and the blessing of our baby making it to full term.

The day had finally arrived when Cruz was born, the waiting room was full of people anxious to meet him. He made an impact on people's lives from the beginning. I wish I could tell you all the details about Cruz and the beautiful ways the Lord created him to see the world. He uniquely saw things, and the Lord used that to impact people. He encouraged his grandpa before his knee surgery, quoting his favorite verse. "Do not be afraid for I am with you" (Isaiah 43:5). He comforted his grandma by showing up when she needed him most, as she was losing her mom, his great grandma. If he did something kind for someone, he would say,

"I defeated Satan!" He encouraged his great-grandpa by telling him, "You don't need to worry, grandpa, grandma is with Jesus," after she passed away. He often asked, "Do you know Jesus?" to strangers, family, friends, missionaries, and high school students. He had a curiosity about heaven and often asked us all about it. We had thoughts and dreams of the life Cruz would live, and we prayed big prayers for him. We prayed he would impact countless people for Jesus. Two years later, we welcomed Maverick into the family. He brought so much joy, and immediately, Cruz and Mav formed a tight bond that only brothers can have. We were so grateful for our little family and for these moments together.

The Day That Changed Everything

It was a typical day. Ben was at work, and I was home with our boys. Little did we know that in 10 short hours, we would be in an ER fighting for our son's life. Cruz was four, and Maverick was almost two. Mav was having a more challenging day and did not want to nap. As a mom of two little boys, our days sometimes felt long, and that day felt just that way. We decided to make the most of the lack of naptime and enjoy the day. In the morning, we wanted to get out of the house, so we decided to go get donuts. Then, the boys played in the mud, leading to an afternoon bath. Cruz made his little brother's belly laugh the whole time in the tub by shooting water out of his mouth. In the afternoon, we went to the library. By the time we got home, we knew Ben would be arriving at any moment from work. We began looking through our amazing library finds and reading them on our living room floor. Ben got home, and our boys ran to him in excitement. They couldn't wait to show him their books and have him read along with us. We read for a while, and then Cruz said his mouth hurt. We went into the kitchen, and I tried to look in his mouth, but nothing appeared wrong. A few minutes later, he began to throw up. The stomach bug had been going around, so we assumed he also had it. He started to get lethargic because he was throwing up frequently.

We called the nurse's hotline, and they explained that it was normal when they were throwing up so much from the stomach bug. This made us feel a little better and we were hopeful he would be feeling better soon. A few minutes later, Cruz's body began to tense up. We knew we had to get to the hospital. We rushed into the ER, and they quickly got him into a room. Immediately, doctors and nurses filled the room. You may have seen this scene on a TV show, or maybe you, too, have experienced a moment like this. It is intense and overwhelming. It moved so fast. People were in and out, medicine was being given, and tests were being done.

We sat there and held Cruz's hand. We had no idea what was happening, but we kept praying. They did multiple scans to try and pinpoint what was wrong. Then the doctor walked in and said the words we never expected to hear. "He has a brain bleed and needs to be life-flighted to Children's Hospital." Questions swarmed through my head, "How is this possible?" "What does this mean?" "How did this happen?" Cruz was always so healthy. He was rarely sick and never had any health issues. But, there was no time for answers at this point.

Ben and I had to go separately to the nearest children's hospital, about an hour away. The drive seemed to take forever as we quickly tried to get to our boy. When I arrived, I ran into the hospital, and they led me up to his room. I began telling the security guard about my son and his love for Jesus. The security guard didn't say much. I met Ben there, and we went into Cruz's room. He was being prepped for brain surgery. We hugged, kissed, and prayed over him and the doctors. Before they wheeled him out on his bed, I stopped them and said, "This is Cruz. He is incredibly special, loves people, and lives life fully. He loves excavators and monster trucks. He loves telling people about Jesus. We are praying for you and thank you for doing all you can to save our son's life." I wanted them to know that they were about to operate on a very special four-year-old boy. I wanted them to understand who Cruz was and, more importantly, who his Jesus was.

We waited in that waiting room for what felt like an eternity. We prayed, we paced, we waited. We received no updates. We had no idea what was going on. Finally, they came and got us. They gave us very little information but told us Cruz was out of surgery and we could see him soon. Once Ben and I were able to see him, we were in his room for only a few minutes, but the doctors rushed in and took him back into surgery. Because of the urgency, they had no time to explain what was happening to him. Their priority was Cruz. So we watched them wheel him away back into surgery, yet again with no answers and more fear. Hours later, a doctor came in and we could see it on his face that it was not good news. The outcome was unknown, but they didn't have much hope that he would be able to pull through. We began weeping as we faced the darkest moment of our lives. We thought we were going in to say goodbye to Cruz, but we got a glimmer of hope. The doctors probably didn't have hope, but he was still here, so we knew God could still heal.

His Nearness in the Storm

Something happened in that hospital that is hard to explain. Romans 12:12 continued to show up. It says, "Be joyful in hope, patient in affliction, faithful in prayer." This verse became the focus of our lives in that hospital. It is what we held onto. We had people praying outside of the hospital, in the downstairs lobby, in his room, and in the waiting room. That waiting room became a prayer room that was constantly filled with people. Cruz's hospital room became a place of worship. This may sound strange, but God showed up; that is the only way to explain it. Every hour, a group came in, and we prayed for Cruz. We had constant worship music playing. We had incredible nurses who cared for Cruz. We loved telling them all about him and about Jesus.

I truly believed God was going to heal Cruz miraculously. Medically, they could do nothing, but I knew that meant that only God could. We read him books, sang him songs, and would lie with him every night. We spent five days there praying, trusting, and hoping that Cruz would wake up. People all over our city, state, the country, and even other parts of the world were praying for Cruz by name.

A catastrophic loss brings about many different forms of grief. Some moments hit you like a brick wall, where you can't catch your breath and feel like the air is being taken out of you suddenly and quickly. Then, some moments are less intense, but you carry them with you for a very long time. You may even carry this grief for a lifetime. It feels like a pit in your stomach that won't go away. It's a constant pain that sticks around, and you can't shake it. In our story, we have experienced many moments of both.

At this moment, everything changed. We got hit by that brick wall when the doctor came into our room to do the final test to see if he had any brain activity. They turned and gave us the impossible news that he did not. My husband looked at that doctor and said boldly, "This does not mean our God is not great." They had all heard about Jesus from us, and he wanted them to know He is still good; He is still with us, even when we don't understand. We had prayed that Cruz would be healed—and we knew he was. We knew he had woken up to see the face of Jesus. Anything Cruz did, he was all in, full speed and full force. I imagined Cruz running full-on into the arms of his Savior.

After facing the reality that our beautiful baby boy was not coming back home with us, we had to do what no parent should have to do: walk out of a hospital without their child, with an empty seat in the back of our car, and with a piece of our hearts forever shattered. The Lord had to carry us out. We had no strength left in us. He carried us out of that hospital and would take us through the next few weeks and months ahead, where we had to continue to do the unimaginable. The week to follow was honestly a blur. People were coming and going as we planned for the funeral of our four-year-old son. How would we possibly do any of this? My fear of the front row has suddenly become a reality. All I could think was, "This can't be real; this can't be happening." Every morning when we woke up, we were reminded all over again that this nightmare was our reality.

He will meet you in your suffering

Parts of our story often reminded me of Naomi in the book of Ruth. Naomi and her family had to leave their homeland of Bethlehem to get food to survive. While they were gone, Naomi's husband and her two sons died. Returning to her homeland, she says, "I went away full, and the Lord has brought me back empty." In our story, this felt comparable. When something tragic happens, when you lose control, and there are no answers to your 'why' questions, it leaves you feeling empty. Your life will never be the same, and sorrow will forever be your companion. Tragic loss can do this, yet that is where Jesus meets us. He is known as a man of sorrows. He is well acquainted with suffering. He wept with people; He sat with them in their sorrows. In our darkest days, He met us. A beautiful thing about Jesus is, He meets you where you are, with no expectations of you other than as your Father who loves you deeply and cares for you immensely.

We couldn't look a year down the road or even see the next day. All we knew was to take on each moment as it came, second by second, minute by minute. Each day, God gave us the strength to survive. The only way we could make it through such an immense loss was walking through it with Jesus. This wasn't the end of our story, and it wasn't the end of Cruz's story. We knew we had more days ahead of us with Cruz than we would have without him. Because of this, we had a purpose for today. People need to know Jesus, and Cruz taught us to live intentionally because life on this earth is fleeting. John 16:33 tells us we aren't promised an easy life without loss or pain. The Bible is quite clear that this world will be challenging. God had made a beautiful, perfect place for us, and He didn't want it to be this way. Yet sin entered. Our world is full of brokenness and pain, but that isn't because of Jesus. He promises to restore all things and redeem all of the brokenness.

I found myself longing for that day, longing for heaven, a place I knew one day I would be. Yet I was here. We had to figure out how to live in this world of pain while we longed for the day we would be with Jesus forever, when our pain would finally be lifted, and the day we will get to see our sweet boy again.

Living with Pain and Purpose

It's been two years since we sat in the front row. It has been two years of deep grief and intense sorrow. Through it, the Lord has always been present and has never left us to navigate it on our own. God has met us in whatever state we are in, whether weeping on the floor, taking our first trip without Cruz, whether we are at the beach, or mourning another hard anniversary. We have learned that our lives will never be the same. We will forever hold grief. However, I have seen that we can carry other emotions with our grief. Grief will always be present with us, but I can also hold joy. I can experience both at the same time. Early in grief, I didn't think that was possible, but now I can see that experiencing both grief and joy at the same time is a reality.

The grief will always be there in some shape or form because our love for Cruz will forever be there. There will always be someone missing here on this earth. Yet, one day, I won't have to hold both. One day, the grief will be gone. This hope in Christ is the hope we cling to. Revelation 21:4 says, "He will wipe away every tear from their eyes, and death shall be no more, neither shall there be mourning, nor crying, nor pain anymore, for the former things have passed away."

You may have faced a day like this, or there might come a day when you are at a funeral, and you are the one sitting with your back facing everyone. In whatever you carry today, know your heavenly Father weeps with you. He longs with you for the day when all things are fully restored, and death is no more. I encourage you to hold onto this hope. Hold onto Jesus.

Before Cruz entered the world, our prayers were filled with hopes that he would touch countless lives for Jesus. Little did we know that the story that would unfold was far from what we had envisioned. Yet, even amidst the tragedy, Cruz has left an indelible mark on countless hearts for Jesus. From Nebraska to the far reaches of India, Ireland, and Africa, children and adults alike have been touched by Cruz's message. It's remarkable to see the impact of a four-year-old boy, though we would never label it as "worth it" in our own understanding. The tragedies we face in this life often defy logic, and we would give anything to hold Cruz in our arms once more. Yet, amidst the pain, we catch glimpses of God's hand at work. As Cruz found his way into Jesus' arms, we believe he heard the words, "Well done, good and faithful servant." Our four-year-old son understood the purpose of this life as believers was to be a light and share Jesus with others. While our journey remains challenging, our eyes remain fixed on eternity, knowing that Jesus is the author and finisher of our faith, and that even in the most difficult paths we face, God is enough, and we will ultimately be reunited in victory.

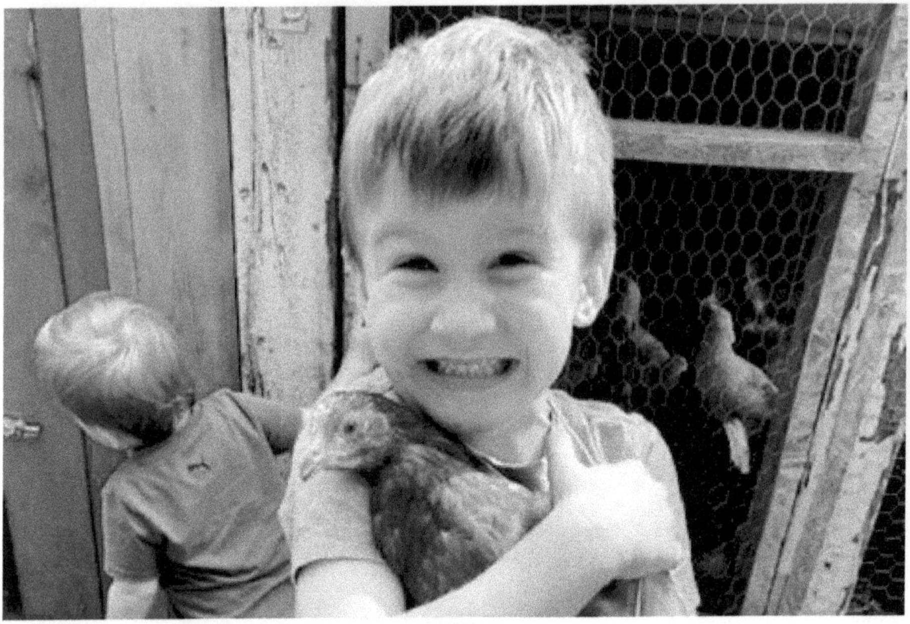

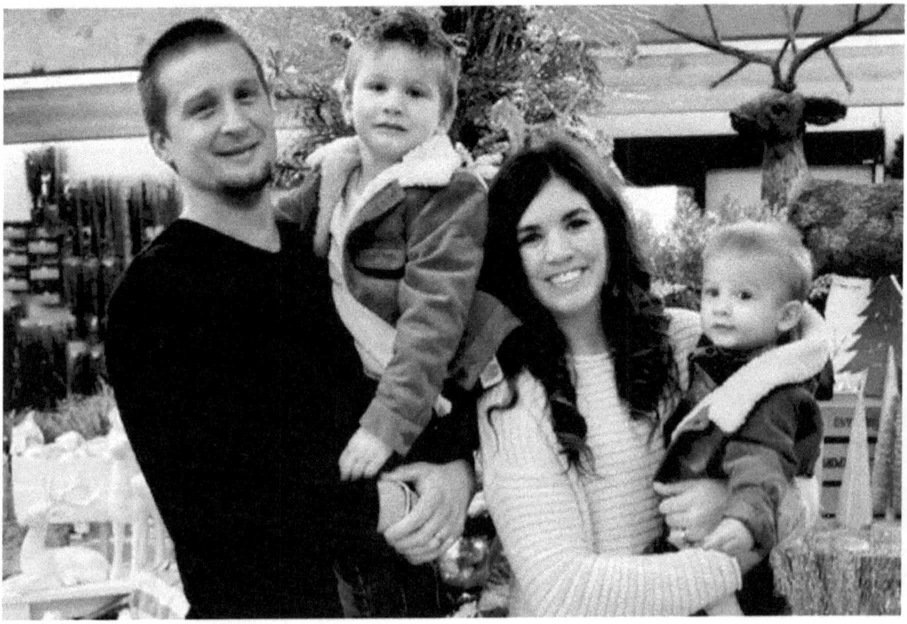

From

Mike and Connie~

Psalm 34:18

The Lord is close to the brokenhearted and saves those who are crushed in spirit.

Even in the depths of our deepest despair, God chooses to draw near to us. He sees our brokenness, understands the depth of our sorrow, and walks with us through the valley of death. It is a profound comfort to know that, no matter how dark our hours may be, God will never leave us. His presence is a constant, gently guiding us through the long, hard journey of loss, offering strength when we feel weakest and hope when the path ahead seems uncertain.

Deidra

By Debbie Blackmon,
Her Mother

Early Childhood

I feel it is important to tell you a little bit about my childhood in order for you to understand me better.

When I was eight years old, almost nine, I was taken, along with six siblings, from our alcoholic parents. My older sister and I were placed in a children's home, while the other five siblings were placed in foster homes or were adopted..

It was a challenging experience for a child, so when I felt sad or lonely, I wanted to blame someone for my unhappiness as most children do so, internally, I blamed "the home." They were the ones that took me from my mom and dad, or so I perceived. With age comes wisdom, and as I got older, I realized my parents chose alcohol over being our parents. I did not hate them or blame them, but understood that alcoholism is an illness. Being young, I decided that with a bit of help, they would be okay, and

I was the one to "fix" them. I planned to go and help them when I was old enough to leave the home. Yet as I began to grow and work on myself, I felt God guiding me to lean into Him and stay focused on what He was doing in me. I'm not sure why (perhaps it was God's protection and intervention), but I never did get to help my parents. During the last year of my life in the children's home (before I was old enough to leave), I finally understood that my parents had many chances and opportunities and had made their own choices. Now, I had to make mine, which was to move forward with my life.

Eventually, I realized that as hard as it was to grow up without my parents, God blessed me by allowing me to be taken from them and placed in a wholesome, Christian environment. In this environment, God provided opportunities to learn about Him and His Word. This experience taught me many things that I have carried throughout my life. Some of those lessons were to be content and adaptable, try your best, and be kind to others. Through that lens, I had a burning desire and determination to be the best mother a child could have. I did not know what being a good mother looked like, but I had developed an image in my mind's eye. I wanted to be the mother I believed every child dreamed of having: one who is always there for you, holds you close, reads your stories, and laughs with you. The one who looks in your eyes, tells you she loves you, that you are unique and loved more than you could know. More than anything, I wanted them to feel they mattered, were important, and loved beyond measure. I wanted to give my children a loving Christian mother and for them to never feel abandoned, unloved, or unwanted.

I wish I could say that things fell into place just as I pictured them. But, you know, life happened, and I had to do some growing up. Dreams of being a flawless mom are way smoother in a girl's head than dealing with the real-life adulting stuff. Before nailing the "perfect" mom gig, I had to level up as an adult and a wife. Life's funny that way.

Years later, I was blessed with two children, a boy and a girl. I learned from childhood how important it was to take my children to church and teach them about God. Although there were times when I did not walk closely with God, He never left me. So, it was off to church because that is what God wanted, and I knew it. Watching them grow was beautiful and challenging. The words "hills and valleys" say it well. We had the hills and valleys, which seemed non-stop, as many parents probably feel.

Deidra was born on August 8th. She was absolutely beautiful! I'm not just saying this as her mother; she genuinely was! Deidra was very independent from the beginning. She walked early, basically potty trained herself, and was very adamant about what she wanted to be when she grew up. It was a natural confidence; she always knew who she was. This independence has many wonderful characteristics, but as we all know, sometimes it's challenging in the teen years. She did well in school but later discovered she could have done better if she had applied herself (those were her words).

From an early age, Deidra had a love and fascination for animals. Even when she began to talk, all she could talk about was getting a horse. When Deidra was in second grade, she asked if we could get a horse. We discussed that our backyard needed to be bigger for a horse to live in. One day, she came home from school and explained she had found a place close to the elementary school where we could keep a horse. Puzzled, I asked how she found it, and to my surprise, she had left school (as a second-grader) and walked across the street where there were horses. This was Deidra, my independent daughter, just doing what she wanted. Still, we had a good discussion about never leaving school (especially since the teachers did not know), crossing a street by herself, or walking up to a strange house. She had reasoned that since I had explained our yard was not large enough, she had to find a place for her horse. And since the one she saw had horses, it didn't matter if it was just a tiny fenced-in mud hole. In Deidra's mind, it made sense that she could get a horse because now she had a place to keep it. Oh, how wonderfully determined she was.

Deidra graduated high school at age seventeen when computers were the latest and most popular career choice. Deidra decided she could make money doing that, so she got an associate's degree in computer networking. It was a short career. Deidra told us that making money meant nothing if you didn't enjoy what you were doing. So, she changed her focus and took extra science classes at several colleges to help increase her chances of getting into Texas A&M Veterinary School. True to form, my independent daughter applied to Texas A&M and got accepted on the first try. She worked tirelessly, came home on holidays, and worked at a veterinary clinic. She saved her money to help pay for the next semester and then returned to school. She worked between classes and on weekends, putting up fences, house-sitting, and caring for people's pets to earn money to pay for school. She was a hard worker and reached her goal of becoming a veterinarian.

Deidra never stopped to whine or complain; she just worked harder. I loved that about her. Deidra was happiest when she worked at saving animals' lives. Seeing the joy on her face as she worked is still one of my favorite memories. I could not have felt more proud of Deidra. I saw her coming into her own, finding her happy place in life, and loving it. She had started visiting churches, and I saw the growth and maturity in our relationship, one I had always dreamed of sharing with her.

I thought being removed from my parents as a child was tough, but I know now it was to help me learn about God and help me become a stronger person. I had no idea the world had much more to throw at me. In one second, all of Deidra's dreams were gone.

The Phone Call

On March 3rd, my daughter Deidra, at 33 years of age, was murdered. It was a senseless murder when two young people, who had been doing drugs, drove by her car and shot into it five times. One of the bullets hit her in the back of the head. I received a phone call saying that Deidra had been shot in the head while she was driving. With no further information, and my husband out of town, my son and I frantically drove to the hospital where they had taken her. There we sat, waiting for them to help her, not knowing what exactly had happened, how she was, or what to expect. We waited silently for what seemed like an eternity.

I'm not sure if it was a nurse or doctor who came out to give an update, but the first words from his mouth were, "I am so sorry we were unable to save her." Now I understand what the statement "the silence was deafening" means. I sat there in the hospital, a thousand miles away, just staring, not sure if I was feeling anything or just dead. After a short period, the doctor came out and said he had a few questions. He asked if I could give any identifying marks that Deidra might have to verify that it was, in fact, "her" they had pronounced dead. After I answered, he turned to leave. I asked if I could see my daughter to say goodbye. His response has run through my brain a million times, "I don't think that would be a good idea. There is blood and brain matter all over the place. You don't want to remember her this way."

As the haunting thoughts played over and over in my mind, and emotions rolled in every direction, I impossibly tried to process what had happened and look for answers. In situations like this, we all must process it in our own time and in our own way. For me, it was easier to move at a slow pace, trying all the while to keep breathing. It would have been much easier to quit trying, but somehow, I knew it would not help my situation, my family, or anyone else, and it would not bring Deidra back.

I chose to talk to God and ask him all the hard questions. I am not happy to admit that I did not turn to Him because He was the Lord of my life. I knew of Him, but did not really and truly know Him. Through this journey, I learned a gigantic difference between the two.

I turned to Him because I was empty. I had no one and nothing that could help me at this point. I have never felt so lost and alone. I needed someone to bear my soul to and be honest about my innermost feelings. Someone who could help me understand what I was feeling. Something, anything, that I could hold onto.

God listened to me no matter how angry I was, the questions I asked, or my railing accusations. He was there listening and sending me small thoughts and ideas to help me try to make sense of all this. Yes, I asked all the questions like "Why me?" and "Why did she have to die?" I laid every possible question at his feet. Some of them were not worded very reasonably, like "Why didn't you....?", "How could you...?", etc., and yet He let me ask.

God answered many quickly and others slowly. Again, God knows when we are ready to hear the truth. He knew I needed small bits of information and time to process and find some understanding. I learned that to move forward, or move at all, I had to have patience, hope, and trust to find peace amidst this tragedy. I have found answers with the help of caring people who met me where I was and let me move at my own speed as I learned to trust God and His infinite wisdom and love. Did God give me yes and no answers immediately? He did not, but He gave me enough hope and knowledge to continue growing and living, looking forward to a future where I will see Deidra and my Lord. Through His hope, and as I grow, I am getting resolution.

The Trial

As time crawled slowly, the trial began. It continuously reopened my raw emotions and wounds. I honestly cannot put into words the pain of losing your child and then having to keep reliving the scene over and over. It's a torment and punishment that only the most evil could curate. For nearly two full years after Deidra's death, we were dealing with the trial and legalities of what had happened. We were going to court and hearing the details and excuses for her murder. Over and over, we sat in the courtroom and listened to the horrible details of what happened to my daughter, Deidra. In my mind, this was so unnecessary; he was guilty, and the case was closed! Both individuals were in custody, and the young man had confessed to shooting at Deidra's car.

I don't remember every detail of each "stage" of the trial. Perhaps that's how God made our bodies to cope with trauma— by allowing some things to blur with time. What I do remember is how incredibly difficult it was to hear the gut-wrenching details day after day. As the trial unfolded, there were small pieces of information that, at the time, were hard to process. But over time, those pieces became like tiny stepping-stones—little by little helping me find some understanding. Looking back, I can see how even the most painful moments were part of God's gentle guidance, leading me toward some comfort and clarity, even in the midst of the chaos.

Shortly after the trial started, I was invited by a group of ladies to join a Bible study on the book of Job. This group of ladies had also each experienced the loss of a child. I had not been in any study group and had no plan of being in one, so why did I accept this invitation? I'm not sure. I was on emotional overload. I felt lost. I was physically, mentally, and emotionally a wreck. Honestly, I was not sure I would make it through the day, so why would I add a Bible study to my plate?

At that time I could not even fathom giving you an answer, I had none. But now, without a doubt, I know it was God sending me angels as people to walk through this tragedy with me. Women who also had lost a child, maybe in different ways, some recently and some a long time ago, but they had walked this road. They were there to support each other and allowed me to bring my raw, unimaginable pain to the group. I remember going to the class more than once and thinking, "What are you doing?" I had difficulty getting out of bed and functioning through each day. I was an emotional wreck, bouncing from overwhelming sadness to being in a zombie-like state. I went from anger, frustration, loneliness, and feeling lost and empty to just uncontrollable crying at any time.

At that time, I wondered, "What am I doing, and why this?" Now, not one ounce of me does not believe it was God who was there helping me cross the abyss that threatened to swallow me whole. Today, I look back and am so grateful I did not turn my back on this opportunity. I can't tell you what we studied, but there were many meetings where the topic spoke to me and what I was going through during the court/trial phase. The women let me lay my raw, wounded heart before them without judgment or fear. They surrounded me with understanding and encouragement to keep going forward. Did they tell me what to feel, do, or say? No. They made me feel loved, cherished, cared for and understood because they also had suffered such pain. I felt God placed me there to give me the courage and strength to lean on Him and continue walking through this valley with the hope of life on the other side.

When the trial finally ended, I felt some relief knowing the man who had murdered my daughter would not be able to do the same to another mother's child for many years. But I still had to face holidays, birthdays, celebrations of marriages, and the birth of children and grandchildren, knowing I would not be celebrating any of those things with my precious daughter.

I know people say "It will get easier with time," and in many ways, it does. Still, during celebratory gatherings and events, I feel that to be not so true. I will confess the edges are not as raw, but the big gaping hole, the void, her absence, has become more solidified in our lives and hearts. "The new normal," as some have called it, is not normal nor what I want normal to be, but it is reality. A specific event, celebration, or even a comment can trigger the memories crashing on me like a giant wave rushing in, making me feel off-balance and out of control. As time continues, I experience the large waves getting smaller and coming less often, making me more stable and able to recover quicker.

Don't get me wrong, the pain and memories are still there, but I have chosen to look at the blessings I have in my life. I hope to see what God will do with this tragedy and turn it into a blessing. I realize He is the only one who can. I am not able to, so I will have faith and trust that good things come from my daughter's death.

After her death, I received many comments and notes from people I had never met. These were not mere condolences. These notes were shared with me to highlight what they believed about Deidra, who was tragically taken from the world. It brought immense joy to my heart. Through their perspectives, I witnessed and experienced Deidra's internal beauty, how she deeply cared for others, and observed her growth into a compassionate and loving young lady. Rather than dwelling on what "can't" be, I now focus on what I was allowed to experience with her and the memories I have and will always cherish.

Earlier, I mentioned things God has done to help me find understanding and growth through this journey. I want to explain more about how I now see He has been with me throughout my life, even before I knew who God was. I will start with Deidra's death because it was a significant factor in my knowing God and learning I could trust Him. Again, I didn't have a revelation all at once with a bright light that made everything suddenly clear. No, He walked me gently through this valley. There were small stepping stones that were helpful thoughts, comments, or events that happened, giving me glimpses of hope. I definitely was an emotional wreck and not sure if I would ever recover. There were so many times I wanted to curl up, cry, and give up. Those times were many, but I knew deep in my heart that it wouldn't be profitable for anyone. But most importantly, I knew Deidra would never want me to give up. She was a fighter with a determination that would not stop, no matter the circumstances. I wanted to make her proud.

On the days I gave in to this way of defeated thinking, I was miserable, and nothing seemed good. So, I would take one more step on each stone, opportunity, or thought and try to move forward. When the horrible thoughts of "how" Deidra died and the horrific comments that I listened to in the hospital and trial would ring through my brain, tearing my heart, I began to hear God's answers. The little bits of information I learned during the trial became stepping-stones to help me process and find some understanding of what my brain was having problems comprehending at the time. The doctor's comment about "the brain matter being all over the place and the large amount of blood loss" many times tormented and overwhelmed me with feelings of emptiness and hopelessness. But later, they helped me feel comfort as I realized this was God guiding me towards understanding that her death was quick and Deidra had not suffered.

As badly as I wanted my daughter to live, I began to look at the reality of things. If Deidra had lived, as I prayed and asked, her injury would have resulted in her living in a vegetative state or being physically and mentally unable to function. That would have been a fate worse than death to Deidra. The letter from the organ donation organization reaffirmed that Deidra's death was instant. They thanked us for our generosity and informed us they were unable to use any of her organs because the blood loss was so quick that the organs failed to be viable. Her body shut down completely when hit with the bullet. When I first got the letter, I again asked, "Why? Why couldn't her death have some meaning?" Later, this was healing for me, and knowing she had not suffered meant the world to me.

I promise it has taken many years for me to write these words, and I must give the Lord credit for it all. I believe He gave me stepping-stones all along the way to help me come to reality with His guidance. Recently, while clearing out some of Deidra's things, I came across a doctor's report that had a cancer result on some tests she had before she died. At first, I panicked, "Why had she not told me? What if..., etc." Then, the calming voice I now choose to listen to reminded me that maybe that was why she died. Perhaps God's mercy prevented her from living through a long, painful illness that ended in death. In it all, I'm choosing to trust Him, even without all the answers.

I have had many opportunities to see glimpses of good things coming from this tragic event. Deidra graduated from college with a veterinary degree three years before she died and was finding her "happy place." She had always wanted to be a veterinarian and was finally enjoying her dream. She was living life to the fullest, helping save animals and making it possible for families to stay with their fur babies. Part of what we do to keep Deidra's memory and dream alive is to help animals survive and keep them with their families, just as Deidra would do if she were here.

I often hear people say, "I HEARD God clearly say..." This has always troubled me some because I kept thinking I was doing something wrong. I talked to Him, asked questions, and waited for answers, but felt like I never heard from Him. Yet as I have spent more time with Him, I must confess I now hear Him speak to me often. Nope, I still do not hear "the voice," but I do believe He speaks to me and has always spoken to me, I just never took the time to really listen. When I needed God most, He sat with me while I grieved, spewed anger, and wandered in circles until the storm inside calmed, and I was ready to listen. I was allowed to hear God's voice through music, especially in my car or when I was an emotional wreck alone in my room. God knew what I needed then and would send me a Christian song with the words, feelings, or sentiments that answered my need. I would often smile, tears running down my face—and boy did that ever feel good! Those moments of peace and relief were oh, so refreshing and comforting. As I have moved further down the road in this journey, music continues to be integral in my healing and growing relationship with the Lord.

Let me encourage those on a similar journey as I close out my story. During the trial, the first two years after Deidra's death, I rode an emotional roller coaster that I wanted off of, but feared I would go into a bottomless pit if the roller coaster stopped. I felt trapped there for the duration. I was grateful for those who visited, but I just wanted to be left alone in my pain. That is not entirely true. I really did not want to be left alone in my pain. I honestly just didn't know how to get out of it. It was easy for me to sit in a pool of pity with hopeless and endless pain. I knew I had to make moves for change, or I might live the rest of my life there. I needed people with hope and love.

I have found hope and love in being around women who lift others up spiritually and mentally. It also helps us physically and emotionally. Maybe because I felt so accepted in the first group, I was willing to take another chance at continuing in another Bible study. Yes, I still felt like a fish out of water. I was still so emotionally raw that if they looked at me wrong or asked me the wrong question, I might fall apart, start bawling, and who knows what else. All of the same thoughts taunted me not to go again. Yet, in His gentleness, God let me know I needed to take the risk and go. I took the risk again and went, and continue doing so to this day. I know beyond a shadow of a doubt that I was led there by an angel (in the form of a friend) sent from God.

Studying God's Word has helped me in every aspect of my life, especially developing a relationship with my Father. I'm so grateful to commonly hear God speak to me now in the little internal voice that nudges me to do something, check on someone, or make a phone call. I'm so thankful that I can truly say I experience the joy of God's nearness. So, take the chance, find somewhere to grow your relationship with God, heal, and bond with others. I promise He will give you stepping-stones every step of the way.

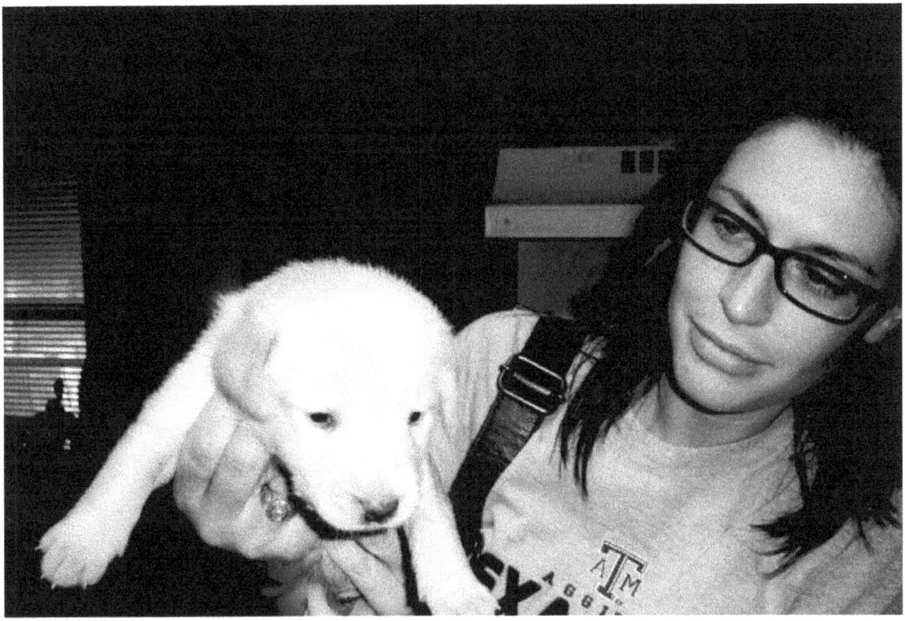

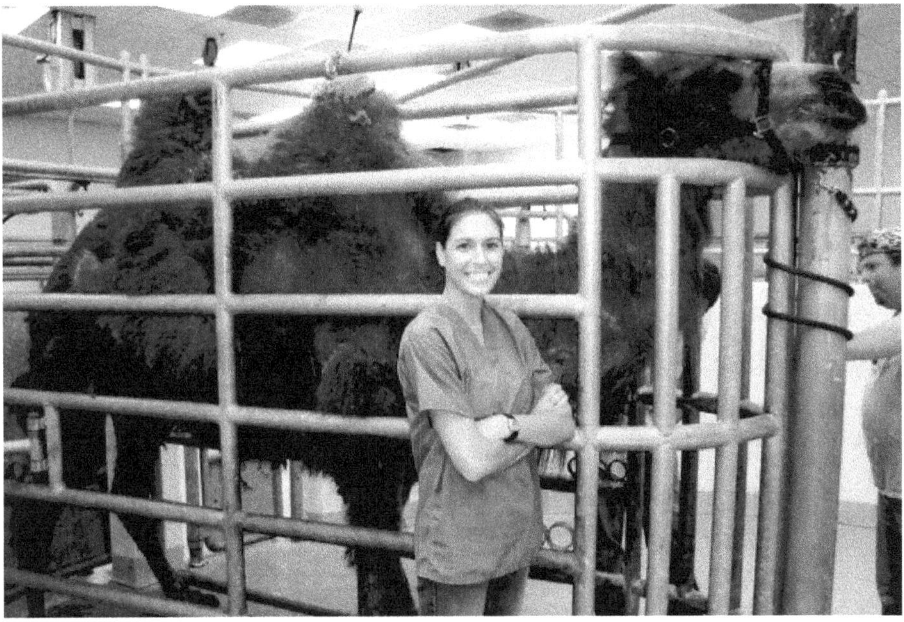

Deidra

From

Mike and Connie~

Isaiah 61:3

*The Lord will bestow on them a crown of beauty
instead of ashes, the oil of joy instead of mourning
and a garment of praise instead of a spirit of
despair. They will be called oaks of righteousness, a
planting of the Lord for the display of His splendor.*

When the weight of loss feels too heavy to bear, and joy seems like
a distant memory, know that the joy of the Lord is still available to
you—and it can become your strength. As a parent who has lost a
child, you may feel broken and lost,, but remember this: You are
called "oaks of righteousness" by the One who created you. That
truth can give you the courage to face another day, even in the
midst of your deepest sorrow. In your grief, you may see yourself
as fragile, shattered by the pain, but God sees you differently. He
sees you as an oak—strong, rooted, and planted by Him for a
purpose beyond what you can see right now.

Without Him, grief can leave us trapped in ashes, consumed
by mourning and despair. But with Him by your side, every step
you take in faith becomes part of a beautiful exchange. He takes
your ashes and transforms them into beauty, your sorrow into joy,
and your mourning into praise. You may not understand how this
can happen in the middle of your pain, but know that through it
all, God is using your journey as a display of His splendor. Even
in your deepest heartache, you are reflecting His glory, and He is
holding you, shaping you, and walking with you every step of the
way. You are not alone in this. He is with you, and He will bring
beauty from the brokenness.

Christy

By Stephen Smith,
Her Father

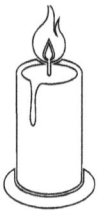

The year 1991 was a huge transition time for our family. We opened a business in June. We had just enough money to make it through the end of the year unless the business turned a profit by December. Unfortunately, the business had not turned a profit, so we were running out of money.

On December 14th, Christy, Andrew, Jody (my wife at that time), and I went to the Flower Mound Christmas parade. I was dressed as Santa Claus, and Jody as Mrs. Claus. On our way home, we passed a burning building at the intersection of Cross Timbers Road and Long Prairie Road. Many people had gathered to watch the burning building because the fire department had set it on fire as a training exercise, jumping in and out of windows and doors. It was an old plant nursery that had gone out of business. Needless to say, the kids were all excited to see it, so I pulled over to the side of the road across the street. Jody and the two kids went over to look at it. I didn't want to get out of the van because I was partially dressed as Santa Claus.

After a while, Jody and the kids were standing at the side of the road, ready to come back to the van. It was just west of a red light. Just as the light turned green, Christy broke away from Jody to cross the street. An acquaintance of ours, distracted by the fire, accelerated from the light and never saw Christy. He ran her down, and she was killed instantly.

It was the worst nightmare of my life. I felt like I was groping in the dark, trying to figure out my next step. I began to question everything in my life—past, present, and future. I wanted to give up; nothing mattered more than our child's life. My family kept encouraging me to just put one foot in front of the other, and keep moving forward. While I have a strong will, the reality of losing our beloved Christy was more than I could handle. I became weak mentally and physically. At that point, nothing was important—only the life of Christy. The finality of death smacked me in the face.

Because I had the Christian knowledge of heaven and hell, I began to investigate if heaven was real. It seemed very important to me to know there was an afterlife and that Christy was in heaven. What happens when a seven-year-old is killed? Do they go to heaven? Christy was brought up in the Christian faith, but at seven, I had to question her personal relationship with Jesus. So I had to know. I started reading the Bible and became convinced that she was in heaven and that there is an afterlife.

Something else happened at the same time. The word of God was telling me to forgive the man who killed Christy. That was the furthest thing from my mind. But as I read the Bible, I saw it again and again. It became a huge burden for me.

One day, we were in court with Doyle, the man who killed Christy. There was a moment when our paths crossed in the courtroom, and I said, "Doyle, I forgive you." He just gave me a stunned stare and kept walking. It was almost as though my body was saying it, but I wasn't sure my heart was in it. At that moment, I felt relief from the burden I had carried. As the day wore on, my relief turned into joy. It was a joy I had never felt before—a kind of metaphysical joy. I realized that the joy emanated from our Father in heaven. Because the Holy Spirit prompted me to obey and forgive, God gave me joy in the midst of the most horrendous experience of my life. How could that be? I then knew I was made to obey Him and experience the unspeakable joy He promises. For me, that moment was a monument marking my rebirth to follow and obey Jesus.

At that point, our house felt empty, so we had two more children, David and Christopher. My life began to change. First and foremost, I wished for Christy's life and death to have meaning and purpose—in my life and in her brothers' lives. I was determined to share the joy of knowing Jesus with the boys as they grew up. In business, we were fortunate enough to reconnect with an old colleague who was willing to pass significant business our way. Our business made a profit and began to grow rapidly.

I began to feel another burden. Our business was successful in a secular sense; however, it was unfulfilling. With the guidance of some acquaintances, we realized that our business could become a ministry. In other words, we could turn the company into a Christian company, with Christian values, a Christian mission statement, chaplains visiting the employees, and supporting other Christian businesses.

We also began to unapologetically share the word of God with employees, vendors, and clients, which was much more fulfilling. So we changed the name from Remedy Staffing to Cornerstone Staffing, naming the company after the Cornerstone of our faith—Jesus. Our mission statement, which appeared on all business cards, read: "Know J.O.Y. in your work"—Jesus first, others second, you third. Our business took off as we attracted tremendous employees, many of whom are still with the company and managing Cornerstone Staffing today. We saw many nonbelievers become believers within the company.

I have since sold Cornerstone Staffing and started a nonprofit, Bible in the Classroom. I now spend most of my time introducing a Bible curriculum to public school districts, and my boys live with the Holy Spirit in their hearts, thanks to Christy's life and death—my blessing in disguise. I continue to fervently read the Bible to understand how Jesus wishes me to live my life. I am like a baby yearning for its mother's milk, as described by Peter. I can't get enough of God's Word.

I have found a new purpose. I now see how Christy's death, though the greatest tragedy of my life, turned into something unexpected. Ten years later, as I listened to the song "Blessings" by Laura Story, it hit me: God had used my greatest pain to bring blessings into my life and my children's lives. Through Christy's life and death, I found a relationship with Jesus.

Finding blessings in the middle of deep grief seemed impossible at the time. But as I worked through my grief, I began to see the hidden blessings God had placed in my life. As harsh as it sounds, it took losing my daughter to spiritually wake me up. I was headed for destruction, but God saved me. Slowly, I could feel His presence and His overwhelming love for me. And with that love came a joy that no one could take away.

I'll close with a few lines from *"Blessings"* by Laura Story:

"What if your blessings come through raindrops?
What if your healing comes through tears?
What if a thousand sleepless nights are what it takes to know You're near?
What if trials of this life... are Your mercies in disguise?"

Christy

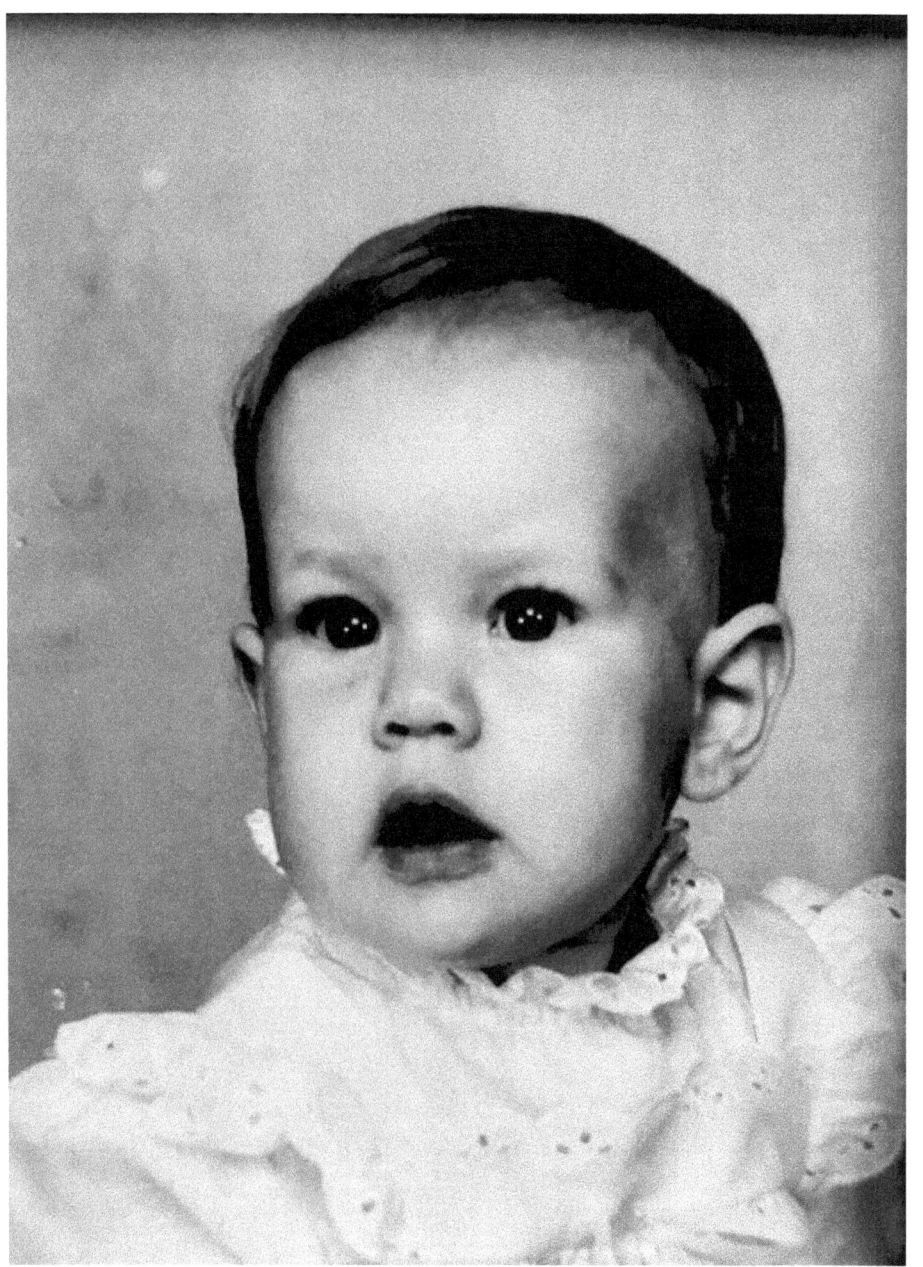

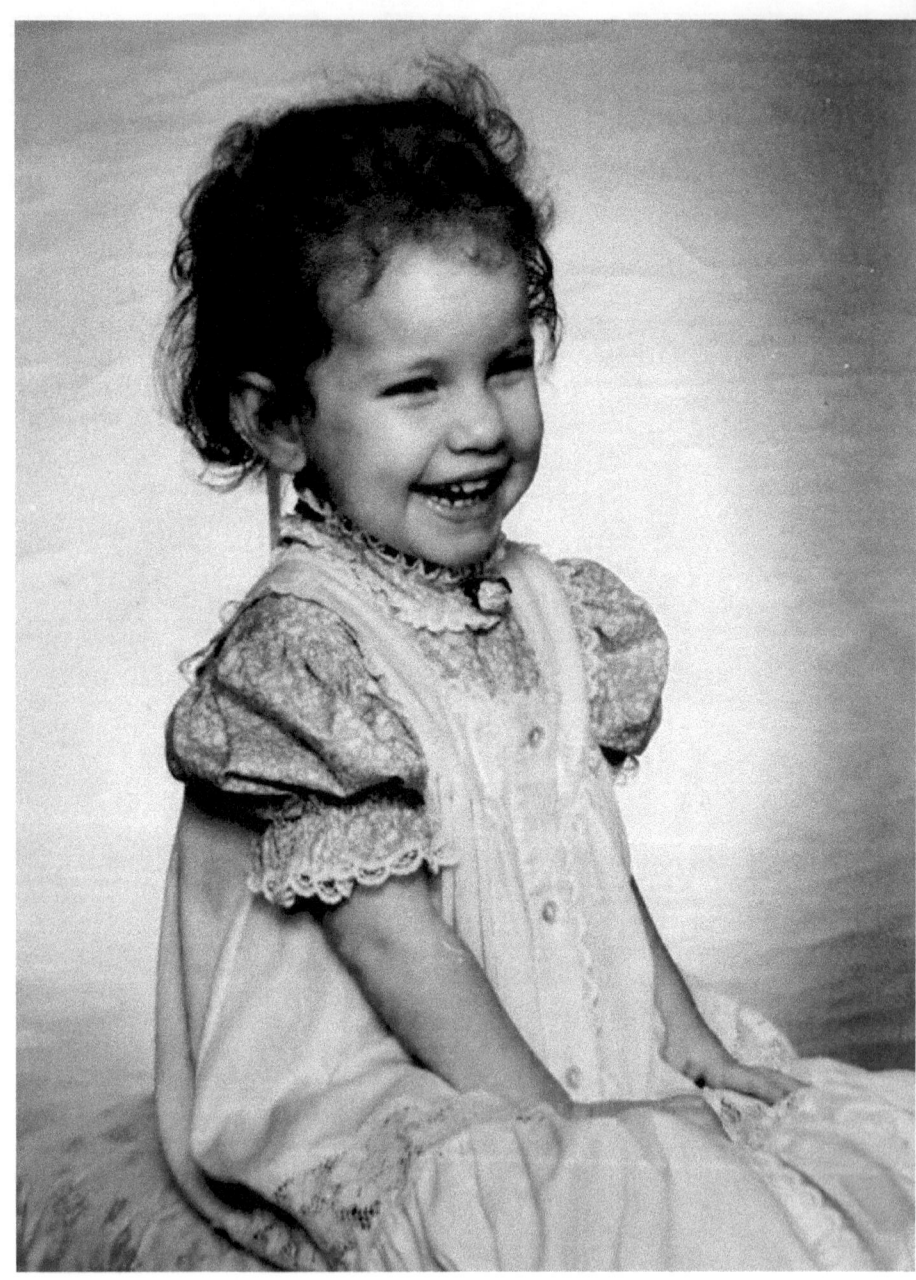

From

Mike and Connie~

Psalm 30:2-3 (NASB)

Lord my God, I cried to you for help, and you healed me. Lord you have brought up my soul from Sheol; you have kept me alive that I would not go down to the pit.

When we find ourselves in the deepest pit of anxiety, fear, and grief—especially after the loss of a child—we must hold onto the truth that God is always ready to heal the brokenness within us. He stands ready to lift us out of the pit, to give us the strength to move beyond our pain, and to help us live a life that honors Him for His unwavering faithfulness.

No pit is too dark, and no wound is too deep for God's redeeming love. Even in our deepest sorrow, He is at work, bringing healing and hope. His grace is bigger than our pain, and His love will carry us through. You are never beyond His reach. His faithfulness will see you through, and He will guide you toward a future filled with His peace and purpose.

Connor

By Nan Deals,
His Mother

We were blessed with a home full of laughter and shared dreams, especially with my trio of boys, Braden (14 years old), Connor (12 years old), and Brennan (10 years old). Connor, my middle child, had a mind that flourished in the realms of creativity. He was right-brained and artistically creative; he found solace in fiction, fantasy, music, and movies. He was an introvert with a beautiful voice that shone when he sang, even though he didn't like the spotlight. The three brothers reveled in their shared love for each other as friends and guarded that fiercely. The oldest two brothers, Braden and Connor, were highly creative, while Brennan leaned more into sports. Connor was adamant that he would be the next George Lucas and constantly shared his story-boarded movie ideas. Our home was fun, full of friends, creativity, and adventure.

Connor's love of music bonded him and me at church. He would always sit to my right at church. He sang tenor, and I sang alto, and we naturally harmonized so well. He would always sit next to me at church, and we would share our love of music as we blended our voices in the songs. The way we were able to harmonize in music symbolized the special bond we had. I love all my boys equally, but Connor and I had this unspoken connection that was sweet and cherished. We got each other.

I remember our last vacation together in the Grand Canyon. As Ron, my husband, and the other boys were climbing dangerously by the edge, Connor and I strolled arm-in-arm that day. He shared his fears of middle school, his heart for a girl, and his dreams of making movies. Like Mary, I treasured all those things in my heart. We looked at life through a similar lens, and I cherished each moment with him. He was also my biggest cheerleader! Once, I performed in a play in Amarillo, and Connor practiced my lines with me repeatedly, never tiring or criticizing. We performed the play eight times in a row, and Connor was there watching every one of them and showering me with praise afterward. He was my son who saw magic in everything creative, and we connected on a unique level in the arts.

Little did I know a storm was brewing beneath the surface of our beautiful life. In February, illness struck Connor, manifesting in troubled breathing and a croupy cough. I took him to Urgent Care, and they gave him a breathing treatment and sent us home. Connor and I stayed at home the next day, and he still didn't feel great but was not running a fever. That night, he asked if he could sleep in my lounge chair by our bed. Connor woke me the next morning, whispering, "Mom, could you help me go to the bathroom? When I went to touch him, he was burning up. He had a fever of 105. My husband Ron had to carry him to the car, and we rushed him to the Emergency Room.

Pneumonia had taken root in one lung, making every breath a struggle. Connor was immediately admitted to Amarillo Hospital, where they intubated him, treating flu on top of pneumonia with a barrage of antibiotics, x-rays, and tests. The doctors there knew he needed better care at a children's hospital, and we began desperate prayers for a bed to open at Dallas Children's Hospital. Before we knew it, a bed had opened. The hospital flew Connor and me from Amarillo to Dallas with the medical team. Ron and the boys would drive to Dallas. The entire transfer was nerve-racking, and it would take 4-5 hours to stabilize Connor.

After they got him from his bed to the medical flight gurney, the flight attendant turned to me, looked me in my eyes, and asked if I understood the severity of the flight. I think she was trying to tell me how delicate he was, and she knew he might not make it to Dallas. But in my mind, I was saying, "Yes, I understand, but do you understand? We prayed for a bed to open up, and it did, and now we are going to Dallas." We prayed, and everything would be ok.

By the time we got to the hospital, Ron and the boys were arriving simultaneously. After initial tests at Children's Hospital, we also found out that on top of the pneumonia, Connor was fighting MRSA, a type of staph infection that is resistant to many antibiotics. Day by day, I stood by him through chest X-rays and CAT scans, essential lines, and treatments. Still, the ECMO bypass machine, a lifeline for his lungs, was a line I couldn't cross; I did not stay for that procedure. It was grueling as a mom to see him this way. They put him on ECMO because of the critical care he needed to let his lungs heal and his body fight the MRSA. We knew this was necessary and settled in for a guesstimated six-week period at the Ronald McDonald house.

I began journaling at the hospital in Amarillo as soon as they intubated Connor because I realized he was missing days. I wanted him to know what had been happening to him and who had come to visit. So, I tried to write as much as I could. I talked and sang constantly to him (per the doctors, we knew he could hear). Ron and the boys whispered in his ear and laid their hands on his chest. He knew we were there. The doctors were encouraged that he was responding to the ECMO and slowly pulled him out of the induced coma. We witnessed tears streaming down his face as we spoke to him. His hand grasped mine, holding on to the world with a fragile grip.

On the tenth day, the staff insisted that I take a break. Of course, I resisted that because I wanted to be with him constantly. However, some friends had come to visit us, and since I had not showered or eaten hardly at all, I agreed to a 30-minute lunch that would refresh me. We returned to the hospital and found Connor's room empty; even the mattress was gone. I ran screaming down the hall, demanding someone tell me where he was. The nurses told us Connor was taken for chest X-ray scans, but I knew the X-rays were scheduled for tomorrow. Panic set in. The nurses said my husband and I needed to meet with them in the consulting room. Those words felt like a knife to my chest; I did not want to go into any consulting room.

We were both taken to the consult room. As soon as the doctors came in, I saw on their faces what they were going to tell us, and I did not want to hear it from them. I ran out to be with Connor. Ron looked puzzled, and asked "Hear what?" He stayed to listen. They told him Connor was dying, and we had only a few hours left with him because he was bleeding in his brain. The MRSA had taken over his body, ravaging every organ. Ron then had the awful job of going and telling Braden and Brennan their brother was dying.

The doctors told us we had about two hours to be with Connor. On February 17th, we spent those two hours loving on our boy. We surrounded him, singing him home to Heaven. It was a sacred moment, bittersweet and full of grace. I know now what a gift it was to be with Connor when he went home because not all parents are that fortunate. After he passed, I couldn't leave his side, touching and kissing every inch of him. Finally, I saw my husband standing at the threshold of the door, gently reaching his hand towards me. My soul felt as it were being torn apart. He was telling me we had to leave. I couldn't go. How could I leave my beautiful boy? It was the most challenging step of my life. At the tender age of twelve, our Connor was with Jesus, and I was left here without him.

In the aftermath, I grappled with my faith journey. Raised in a non-Christian home, I found God in high school through Ron, who led me to the Lord. Ron and I dated, and then he became my beloved husband. But now, with the loss of Connor, my faith was shaken. I cried hard for two years. In the dark, heavy, first days of grief, I wrestled with anger, doubt, and what had happened to my life. My past abandonment issues from childhood and abandonment from Ron (from over a decade of his workaholism) now collided with a massive feeling of abandonment from God. It really was the straw that broke the camel's back. What started as a small glass of wine at night and a sleep aid, morphed into a full-blown addiction.

I rejected the comfort of Scriptures and songs, resenting a God who seemed to have forsaken me. Depression, already present before Connor's death, intensified. I numbly navigated a toxic mix of over-the-counter medicine, prescriptions, alcohol, and poor self-care. My grief was messy, a turbulent sea of anger and despair.

Although Ron's faith wavered, mine overtaken by bitterness. We grieved together for four years, but then Ron read the book of Job and found comfort and hope again. On the other hand, I wore a mask, hiding behind isolation and unkind words. I rejected any light, unwilling to find beauty in the ashes. Trust issues festered, and the enemy found a foothold in my grief.

When Ron found hope, I felt abandoned once again by him, leaving me in my complex, hopeless grief. I led a double life, isolating myself at night with my numbing and coping mechanisms. Most of my numbing was after Ron went to bed. He knew I was drinking, but did not know the extent of it. I hid it from him, my family, and my friends. With my pain hidden in the dark, I clung to being a great mom to my other two sons during the day. I taught school daily and sought solace in my numbing habits at night. I was caught in a vicious cycle, with menopause adding to the whirlwind a storm of its own. Some who know my story would say I was an incredible actress; the enemy definitely used isolation and secrecy.

But in the midst of my mess, God met me.

It was the beginning of my Ephesians 2:4-5 "But God" story.

> *But because of His great love for us, God, who is rich in mercy, made us alive with Christ even when we were dead in transgressions—it is by grace you have been saved.*

***

For eight years, I was consumed with grief, numbing pain, and isolation. There was no light in my heart. Although I taught at the school, attended church, and was a good mom, I was a wreck on the inside. In secret, I was drowning myself by anesthetizing my pain so I could cope with Connor's death. Before then, I was quick to judge others who struggled with anxiety, suicidal thoughts, or addictions. Now, I understand where pain can lead you, and the worst judgment of me came from myself. I had spiraled into a pit so deep I could not see out of it, not even a glimmer of light. The worst part was, itI was in a dark cycle, repeating over and over and over.

In 2017, Ron and I entered the phase of being empty nesters. While he was frequently away on business trips, the strain of alcohol and prescription drugs took its toll, exacerbated by my chronic insomnia (which I now know was spiritual warfare), which kept me awake every hour of the night. Eventually, everything reached a breaking point, plunging me into utter darkness. It was this season that I felt overwhelmed by dark spiritual attacks and the presence of the enemy. I succumbed to his deceitful whispers and believed his lies. By day, I put on a facade while teaching school, where I excelled in guiding five- and six-year-olds. But each evening, I retreated into the depths of despair. I was merely surviving, devoid of the truth and solace offered by the Holy Spirit.

In January 2020, I looked in the mirror and thought, "God, can you help me? I guess I need rehab." I was desperate for peace but tormented by the one who seeks to kill, steal, and destroy (1 Peter 5:8) with the lie, "If you go to rehab, you will destroy your husband's career." I was about to hit rock bottom. Yet God was orchestrating my deliverance, even in the dark. In February, I heard Julie Slattery speak on one of our Family Life trips. God had listened to my weak question, and the first light came into my desperate soul. Julie's words convinced me to ask another wife for help, but the darkness was still intense.

One weekend, before Ron left for a five-day trip, he told he would be unavailable, which triggered me into a tailspin. It was also the weekend the world shut down due to the Covid-19 pandemic. It was no coincidence. I know now that God used Covid for my rock bottom. I had no kids living with me, no job, and no friends to visit or have dinner with. I was utterly alone and felt absolutely abandoned. I went on the biggest bender those five days, drowning myself with alcohol and drugs.

In desperation, I literally called Ron 50 times, texted him 50 times, and called my boys threatening to harm myself. I had hit the absolute bottom. When Ron got home that Sunday night, I could tell by the look on his face he had had enough. I was terrified for my marriage. He looked at me and said, "Nan, who are you? Who acts like this?" His words shook me, but I remember thinking, "I don't know." I was so broken, so shackled, and so lost and full of shame. The following day, Ron got up to get on a call with his team to figure out how to do his job in a pandemic. Once again, I felt utterly alone with nothing–no husband, no job, no children. But God was still there.

It was March 16th. I was home because of the pandemic. I went into our guest room and got out my yoga mat to stretch. I laid down and started crying, crying so hard, like the guttural cries at the beginning of my grief. I could not get up and lay there in the waves of gut-wrenching tears for two hours. The words tumbled out of my mouth, "God, I can't do this on my own. I need you. I hate myself. My heart is as black as coal, but if You will have me... could you change my blackened heart and make it new?"

It was a moment of surrender. I finally surrendered my life on that yoga mat. I had nothing left, but God was enough. It was as if God stood me up, wiped me off, and said, "Now I can work with this. I have been waiting for you, sweet girl." Oh, the sweetness of our Lord. He had simply been waiting for me to surrender and met me in my mess.

That day, I searched on my phone's music app for the words "Create in Me," and God downloaded five songs, songs like *Create in Me* by JJ Heller and *My Portion and My Strength* by Ellie Holcomb. I listened to those songs on repeat for six months. I pulled up a Julie Slattery podcast that same day, and she had a guest who talked about praying. I ordered her book, and it came the next day, even during a pandemic. I walked for an hour every day for a month listening to the Dwell app and any Bible teaching I could find. My spirit was waking up with worship and Scriptures, and I was finally letting the light in. My dry bones were soaking it up, and I was coming back to life.

That first night after the yoga mat, I went to bed without any alcohol and just my regular meds (I knew not to do that cold turkey). Astoundingly, I did not have one withdrawal (a grace that I do not deserve, BUT GOD), and my sleep was being restored. The mercy of God was truly unexplainable. God had heard my cries and was pulling me out of the pit.

> *O Lord my God, I cried to you for help, and you have healed me. Oh Lord, you have brought up my soul from Sheol; you restored me to life from among those who go down to the pit.*
>
> —*Psalm 30: 2-3*

See, while I had been in Sheol, He was the Light that had rescued me—even from myself.

It was a slow and steady process. He so sweetly was the lifter of my head. My sister and brother-in-law connected me with a biblically-based recovery program called Regeneration from Watermark church. In this program, God revealed Himself further to me and helped me trust Him with my past pains and fears. God was so faithful, just, kind, and patient. There was so much freedom in confessing my sins to my husband and boys. They met me with such grace and love; I received blessings upon blessings.

I do have true joy now. I remember when I wasn't sure I would ever be able to say that. I remember my anger in that dark season when they sang "It Is Well with My Soul" in church. Yet in May of 2020, I went to Connor's graveside and could say, "Connor, it's not good that you aren't here, but God is good." That was a miracle to me.

I want to tell you that you can give Him all of it: the intense pain, sadness, anger, and heartbreak. I promise you He can take it. Shutting out the Light and living in the darkness of shame and isolation are tools of the enemy. Here, I had built this beautiful legacy for my son, but I was living in shame and perpetual angst, and it was all suffocating. Now I feel made new again. Oh, how surrendering to Him has set me free!

He is a wonderful, merciful Father; God has given me a second and third chance. I have a beautiful new faith and a renewal of my spirit. I genuinely know I can trust Him, and you can trust Him with anything because of who He is. He is a good, trustworthy God who will never leave you.

God restored the years the enemy stole (Joel 2:25-27) in my marriage and family. I owned my stuff with my husband and boys, and there has been a lot of forgiveness and reconciliation. I've had to forgive myself, too. God is continuing to restore my heart, my marriage, and all of my relationships.

I've always had hope and knew I would see Connor again. But it's different now. I long to be in Heaven with Connor (as any bereaved parent does), yet now I long to embrace my Lord and Connor. My perspective is eternal, and I'm living here purposefully. Now, I can stay here and do this life and enjoy it with true joy in my heart. Before, I wanted to bypass Earth. Now I have hope and can live in the light.

I wish my story were clean and tidy; sometimes, it is hard to share. It was isolating, messy, and dark. I share it because I want you to know there is hope. After all, He is Light. There is nothing you can do to make Him not love you. Oh, how He loves you, and

I promise He is a God you can trust to be the lifter of your head (Psalm 3:3).

I'll leave you with some of my favorite verses. I hope you will look them up and they will carry you as they have me:

Psalm 139

Psalm 51

Psalm 103:8-12

Zeph 3:17

Proverbs 3-5-6

From

Mike and Connie~

2 Corinthians 4:16-17

Therefore we do not lose heart. Though outwardly we are wasting away, yet inwardly we are being renewed day by day. For our light and momentary troubles are achieving for us an eternal glory that outweighs them all.

When tragedy strikes, the grief can feel utterly overwhelming, as if it will consume us. No one in the midst of such sorrow would ever say their pain is light or momentary. In those darkest moments, grief feels heavy and endless. But it's only when we gain an eternal perspective—when we look beyond our immediate suffering—that we can begin to grasp the hope of eternal glory that God promises us.

When we compare our trials to the immeasurable glory that awaits us, we start to see our pain through the lens of God's greater plan. While our hearts ache deeply now, understanding the eternal perspective brings comfort and a sense of purpose to our suffering. It's when we shift our focus from the weight of present sorrow to the promise of eternal joy that we begin to find meaning in the overwhelming grief. God's Word reminds us that our suffering, though incredibly painful, is not the end—it is part of the journey that leads us to a glorious future beyond our understanding.

Lindsey

By Jennifer Durham,
Her Mother

✝

*"When there are no words, there is
a warm blanket."*

*"Mom, I found a lump and went to the health
center. They think it might be* **C A N C E R.**
Can you come?"

*It came out of nowhere.
It lasted for three years.
Then she was gone.*

How do I even begin to tell of the many tears and cheers, the sudden turns and the long straightaways, the midnight pacings, the sunrises—and the rainbows? Hope took flight and then was dashed against the rocks so many times. There were times when I deeply felt the presence of Almighty God, and there were also many silent stretches—hours, days, even months—when that sense of His presence seemed like a vast emptiness.

There were moments when prayer provided comfort, and other times when it was just barely breathing the name of Jesus.

And, it was enough, Jesus was enough—and He still is today.

I'd love to tell you about Lindsey!

Born two months premature, after a traumatic pregnancy, the doctor saying, "You realize she is a miracle don't you?" and the nurse saying, "I see so many babies, but she is a beauty."

Lindsey had a light about her, God-given of course, that traveled the 23 years of life with her even through the entire cancer journey. She was a magnet, drawing people in with her enthusiasm, her depth, and her purity. She loved Jesus deeply and showed that love by cherishing her family and friends. She made each person feel special because she had a remarkable ability to see the unique worth in everyone.

Her faith was immense. Her laugh was infectious, her enthusiasm for life never faltered, and her deep understanding of people and the things of God drew many to her during their most defining moments. She lived life fully.

Lindsey was a 20-year-old sophomore at the University of Oregon, majoring in Communication Disorders and Speech Science, with the goal of becoming a speech pathologist like me, her mother. At that time, I was running my large therapy clinic in Medford, Oregon, and I envisioned Lindsey working alongside me there and, if she chose, eventually taking over the clinic. She had a natural gift with children and would have been an exceptional therapist for both kids and adults.

When I got that life-altering call, I was in the middle of a divorce from her father, struggling to keep my upended life together. Standing in the hallway of my clinic, answering her call on my way to see the next patient, time seemed to both freeze and race forward, Cortisol became my constant companion.

I'm not sure how I managed the three-hour drive to the University of Oregon in Eugene that day. I drove in loud silence, but with heart palpitations (which I'd been battling for a year due to stress), dry mouth, and tunnel vision to get to Lindsey. Little did I know this would be just the first of many grueling drives.

I was so overwhelmed that I couldn't even think about eating, which led to frightening weight and hair loss. My constant vigilance meant I wasn't sleeping. Trauma has a way of sinking deep into your bones—a truth I'd known since childhood. But so does the strength and determination of a survivor's spirit, especially the one the Lord built in me through years of walking with Him in trauma recovery. Over my young adult years, I developed a rich set of tools from daily time in my prayer room, studying five different versions of the Bible, and experiencing the Lord's touch on the mountaintops of my faith.

And now, facing my daughter's diagnosis of cancer, I held tightly to what I knew from the Word and relied on that. But I can't say I felt the Lord closer than ever during or after this journey. Many times, I felt like I was standing empty-handed in a spiritual desert. I often found myself saying, "But Lord, I thought I'd feel you closer, I thought prayer would be sensed more powerfully, I thought..."

Even so, I haven't asked the Lord, "Why?"

I find that strange, because I speak with others who have lost children and they describe themselves asking Him frequently, "Why?" "Why my child?" "Why me?" "Why this way?" Of course, they would ask that. I would expect it even from myself.

Why have I not asked "Why?"

I believe that if God wanted me to understand something, He would make it clear and tell me. He doesn't owe me any explanations and, honestly, with my limited perspective, I might not even grasp it if He did. I trust God as God, and recognize that

He doesn't owe me anything. My debt to Him is immense. I start by respecting and honoring Him as the most Holy and High God. For me, it really comes down to that simple truth.

I look forward to the day when I can go home to Him and be reunited with Lindsey. I know that's when I'll finally have complete understanding. For now, I must simply wait.

Lindsey had a contagious laugh. She'd throw her head back and laugh with her whole being. She had an enthusiasm that would blurt out of her at a moment's notice, "Oh, oh! You know what we should do?!" It often involved going for a smoothie, ice cream cone, or chocolate dessert. For Christmas, she asked for gift cards at coffee shops (for visiting with friends) or sandwich shops (for giving to the homeless). She loved to dance.

It was the night before Lindsey was set to start a new, more intense round of chemotherapy, after the first four-month treatment had failed. She had already lost her long, flowing blonde hair and her athletic runner's figure. Despite everything, she refused to wear wigs. She would proudly walk around campus and go out to restaurants with her bald head and now-bony legs. Sometimes, she'd cover her head with colorful scarves or knit hats with pom-poms—she was a cute bald girl. People stared, and I watched them, but Lindsey seemed not to notice; or did she choose not to?

As it got late, we couldn't quite settle in for sleep. I'd travel to Eugene for each of her treatments and doctor's appointments, sleeping on an air mattress beside her bed during the toughest recovery days. She lived in a Christian women's co-op with 40 other Christian girls from the university, and they were a constant support throughout her journey. They were incredible— attending appointments when I couldn't, surrounding her during chemo sessions, and visiting her room to share their own stories. Lindsey never wanted to stop ministering, even while she was struggling. But that night, it was just the two of us, and we were both nervous. Then, in true Lindsey fashion, she jumped up from her bed and decided to clean out her sock drawer—she was always at her best when she kept busy.

While sorting through her things, she found a shirt given to her as a gift with the word "HAPPY" in gold sequins. She put it on and then turned on Pharrell Williams' song "Happy." She danced her way through the entire four-minute track, making me laugh so hard I was in tears while I tried to capture the moment on video. That is who Lindsey was. I cherish those deeply intimate times that she and I had together as a result of Hodgkin Lymphoma.

We'd hold hands; something we hadn't done since she was four years old. We'd sit in the car a long while after parking, reflecting on the moment, and gaining the oomph to crawl out of the car and navigate the stairs to her apartment. We'd get our nails done—something she could still enjoy even when she wasn't feeling great. We'd watch "Frozen" on her laptop while she rested in bed for a few days after tough chemo sessions or catch episodes of *The Bachelor* with her college friends. We had a bedtime ritual every night after turning off the light. Lindsey would ask, "Mom, am I okay?" and I'd respond, "Honey, you're more than okay." We both understood why: because of God.

Scan days were sharply anticipated. Lindsey had her lucky tie-dyed socks she wore for each scan. She was always upfront about how much anxiety she struggled with—it was her biggest challenge. She kept a Facebook page called "Lindsey's Journey," where she shared her daily experiences through her cancer journey with over 1,000 followers who prayed and hoped for her. Last I checked, the page is still up on Facebook. She was so honest, raw, hopeful, and sincere. She posted photos, asked for prayers, celebrated her victories, and kept everyone updated on both the good and the tough news she received.

Lindsey had a remarkable way of reaching out to everyone following her journey, figuratively holding their hands and inviting them to walk alongside her. She welcomed and comforted not just the doctors and nurses, but also family, friends, and even their friends throughout those three years. I often said that Lindsey helped us all through her cancer. She was incredibly wise for her years, so loving, and deeply secure in her relationship with Jesus.

After a difficult multi-week series of chemotherapy, we'd often see promising results in the scans. We held onto the hope that the doctors' initial diagnosis statement—that Hodgkin Lymphoma is one of the most curable cancers, with a success rate over 90%—would prove true. But then, at the next follow-up scan, the cancer would return. More lymph nodes would light up on the images, and we'd have to start over. Her hair had just grown back into a cute, short, spiky style, only to be lost again with an even more aggressive round of treatment. Eventually, a bone marrow transplant became her only hope.

This time, the goal was to get her back into remission with more chemotherapy so they could harvest her own bone marrow. Once that was done, she'd be admitted to the bone marrow transplant unit at Oregon Health Science University. There, she would face the most intense chemotherapy yet—so harsh that it would destroy her own bone marrow and put her in a life-threatening immunocompromised neutropenic state. Finally, they would return her healthy bone marrow to her.

The transplant journey started after more than a year and a half of intense treatments. I was utterly drained on every level—physically, mentally, emotionally, socially, financially, and spiritually. Cancer takes a toll on every aspect of your life. As a mother, I felt each needle and each moment of anxiety deeply. I couldn't afford to fall apart; I needed to stay strong and stable for Lindsey. I had to keep my clinic running and hold everything together. But eventually, the stress took such a toll on me that my whole nervous system was on the brink of breaking down.

By the grace of God, a wonderful man came into our lives. Jim and I married in October, and Lindsey's transplant followed the next October. He became a rock for both of us. Jim arranged for us to stay in a motorhome parked at Oregon Health Science University, so we were close to Lindsey during her treatment in Portland. I was incredibly grateful to have a place that was both affordable and nearby. Jim and I would make the drive back to Medford from Portland to handle our responsibilities, but finances were tight since I couldn't pay myself for months. My clinic started to struggle, and eventually, I had to scale back and close it down. The combined weight of legal, financial, medical, and personal challenges on top of the cancer journey was overwhelming.

Heart palpitations felt like a giant salmon flopping around in my chest, stealing my breath and triggering panic attacks. Dizziness and even diarrhea pushed me to the edge. Was it a nervous breakdown? I'm not sure, but I've wondered. The emergency room staff didn't offer much care or compassion; they just put me in a room and sent me on my way after a dose of Ativan.

We got back to the motorhome at 3 a.m., and Jim left two hours later to return to Medford for his work. There I was, alone again in that big parking lot, feeling utterly weak and defeated. I felt I was failing as a mom, because I had hit my limit when all I wanted was to be there for Lindsey and offer her strength. Soon after, I caught the flu and had to go back to Medford to get antibiotics and recover to make sure I wouldn't risk exposing Lindsey. Leaving my daughter while she was fighting for her life in that hospital bed was heart-wrenching. She underwent many blood transfusions and additional procedures. She became incredibly weak of body, but remained strong of spirit. And after several months in or near the hospital in Portland, she finally went home to Eugene to recover and to hope.

In an amazing turn of events, God brought a wonderful man into Lindsey's life, too. The joy she felt while planning her wedding was truly priceless. We went gown shopping together, and though the sales ladies couldn't help but notice her bald head and thin frame, to me, she looked absolutely beautiful. By her wedding day, a bit of her hair had grown back, and she had enough energy to dance. Unfortunately, the day she returned from her honeymoon, she had to rush to the emergency room to discover that the cancer had returned. Still, she enjoyed one full week of marriage with cancer in the background, rather than at the forefront.

We faced more scans with dwindling hope. The night sweats—a telltale sign of the cancer's grip on her body—had returned with a vengeance. It was scan time again, and we needed to find out if the cancer had come back and how severe it was. Jim and I were on our usual drive up Interstate 5 from Medford to Eugene for the appointment with the oncologist, bracing ourselves for the results and the treatment plan. We'd been through so many of these appointments, but this one felt particularly dire.

Then, just as we were approaching a hill, the car suddenly jerked and failed to accelerate. We ended up stranded on the side of the interstate, 60 miles from our destination, with a broken transmission. If there was ever a lowest moment, perhaps this was it.

I sat in the car, feeling helpless, as I listened to the heartbreaking news on the phone: "Lindsey, the cancer is back and there's nothing more we can do." Hearing her sobbing while I was unable to be there for her was unbearable.

Uncountable scars from chemo ports and central lines, IVs and surgeries littered her once unscathed, young 22-year-old body.

She began having cardiac irregularities, common after intensive chemo, and underwent many echocardiograms. Her lungs began to fill with fluid requiring a Pleurex chest tube to extract the excess and prevent total lung collapse. She developed painful neuropathy in her feet, another common side effect of chemo. Fatigue limited the time she could be up and moving around, so she lived on the couch in her tiny apartment. When she began having difficulty swallowing, we struggled with the decision to have a stomach tube placed for nutrition. Her teeth began to look like oversized dentures as her face became hollow. Her legs were nothing but bones; she walked with a cane to assist with balance. Conversations became too exhausting; her Facebook updates went silent.

She was leaving us.

She wanted to make it to Christmas.

She died one week before on December 18, 2016.

The hospice week was traumatic; something I didn't expect as a HomeHealth and Hospice clinician myself. We were in the middle of an intense ice storm that disabled nurses from reaching us. We even lost the electricity for four days, and sat in the dark with just enough electricity to power Lindsey's bed, her oxygen, and the refrigerator for her medications. Lindsey struggled. With many of her closest family and friends around her, she fought to the end, and her body did not want to let go. Finally, we had to give her the heavy medications that would send her to a state of calm and rest—and close her eyes forever.

How I didn't stop breathing along with her, I don't know. I kissed her on the forehead and she was already getting cold. She was not there any longer. Jim asked to be the one to wrap her body and place her in the body bag the coroners brought. I could not look, but I heard the zipper.

I cannot describe the separation anxiety I faced after they took her. I had been traveling at 200 mph and hit a wall. I could no longer make sure that she was alright! The brain of a mother cannot comprehend her child dying.

Shock is a God-given gift of anesthesia. I walked in that fog-like state for several days, months; perhaps on some level for years.

Now, nearly eight years from saying good-bye, it can still seem like yesterday. Each year has carried its hallmarks of grief. The year of firsts, then the second and third years, when the distance and the missing intensified. The years of "Who am I now?" The years of absence, fatigue, and a sensitive neurological system lingering. And then there's Christmas and her birthday returning each year, as I find breathing to be a chore each time around.

Little by little, I have been able to regain some capacity for doing life. I never stopped working or going through the daily motions, but it was void at times of my being truly present. My identity as a mother, lost.

I deeply miss Lindsey and, with equal depth, miss the me that I was.

One of the hallmarks of grief is loneliness that cannot be filled, because we miss who we were with them in our lives. Grief is deeply physical for mothers, leaving a hole in our being. Perhaps we eventually learn to accept that there is a piece missing within us and live with it. What other choice do we have?

Today, I live in a beautiful house that Lindsey has never seen. I have two cats, Lindsey has never met. I have a little granddaughter who will not know Lindsey. I will face aging without her. She was my only. I am deeply blessed for the 23 years I had with her. As the pain of my happy memories begins to recede, allowing me to enjoy the memories without incapacitating tears, I embrace those memories until I join her. In the blink of an eye, we will be together again.

I remain close with several of Lindsey's closest friends. We host a retreat for them and us each year, to remember Lindsey and what she loved. I watch these women as they buy their first homes and welcome their first, second, and even third babies.

In Lindsey's memory, we began a non-profit called "Warm Blankets." There were many times when I could not offer any help to her discomfort except for a warm blanket. When there were no words, there was a warm blanket. She always had a blanket. She was always cold on her cancer journey; her blankets were her greatest physical comfort.

Our non-profit exists to come alongside those facing traumatic grief and loss and/or facing difficult cancer journeys. We believe in ministry by presence, so we offer simple comforts with our comfort bundles that contain a super soft warm blanket, and other comfort items that we hand-select such as stuffed animals, mugs, Lindsey's favorite tea, beanie hat, neck warmer, chocolate, book of God's Promises, or even financial support for bridging the monetary gap that cancer and loss create.

We have had the privilege of sitting in a hospital or home as others say goodbye to their loved ones, and have been able to respond with simple comforts and listening presence. We prayerfully seek to provide for additional needs that we identify along the way, as well. We have a band that plays a mix of our favorite cover songs and original pieces, along with a recording studio where we create inspirational music to support our efforts. We desire to "comfort others in any trouble with the comfort we ourselves have received from God" (2 Corinthians 1:4).

I have the privilege of leading a small support group of mothers who have also lost a child. Each of us agree that this group has proven to be one of the most beneficial steps taken to soothe our grief, to find meaning in our loss, to reassure us that we are not going crazy, and remind us we are not alone. Finding other mothers who are navigating this tough journey has been incredibly valuable. We lean on each other and find comfort in our being in the hands of God as we deal with the aftermath of loss, which has shaken every part of our lives—mental, emotional, physical, social, spiritual, and financial. We hold on to one another tightly as we move through the seasons of grief together.

Every time I get to comfort others with the comfort I've received from God and share the truth of His Word and promises—which rise above our feelings, doubts, and fears—it brings a bit of healing to my own soul. There have been countless opportunities to do this, as so many people need ministry simply through our presence. If this pain can find purpose, the Lord's purpose, then I will walk in the pain.

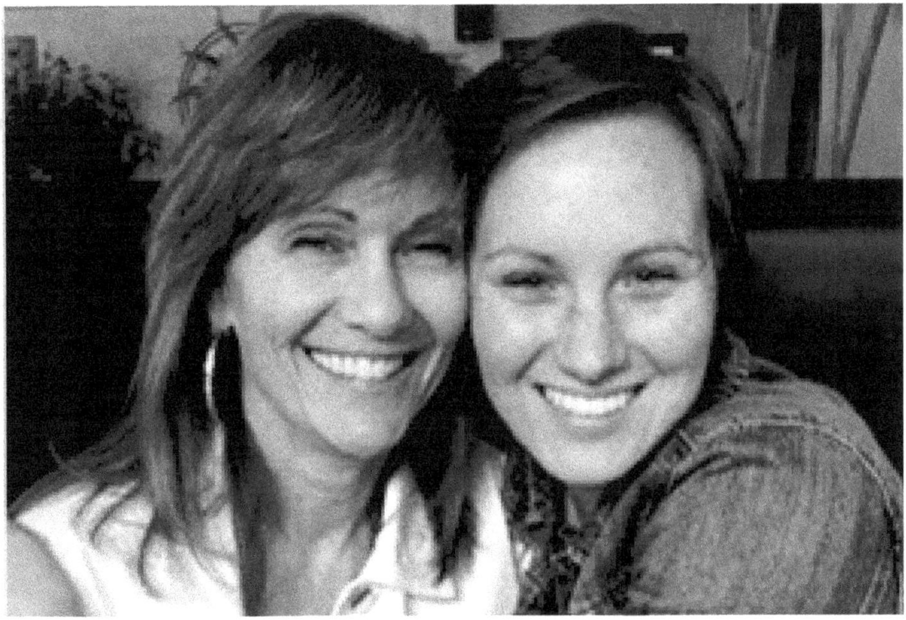

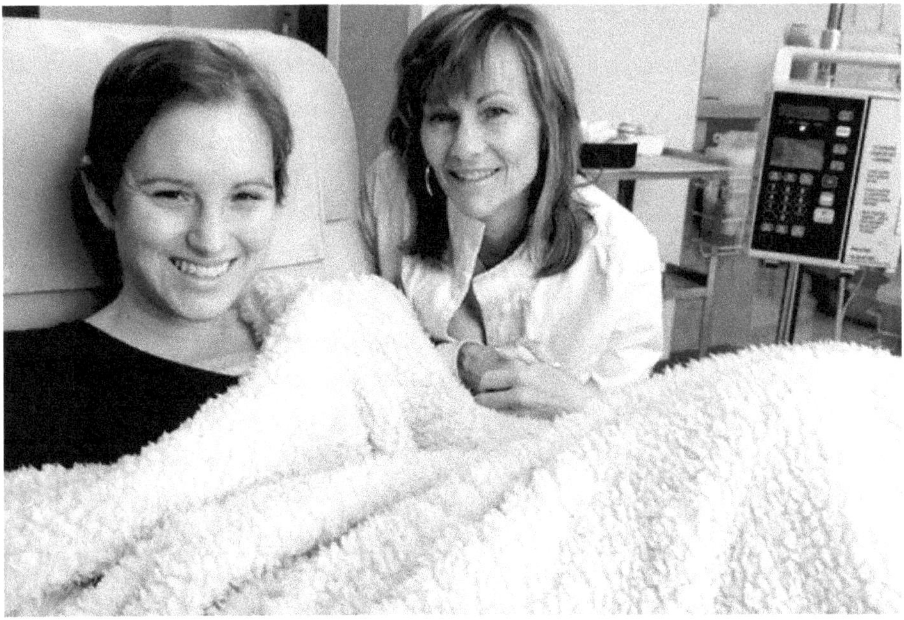

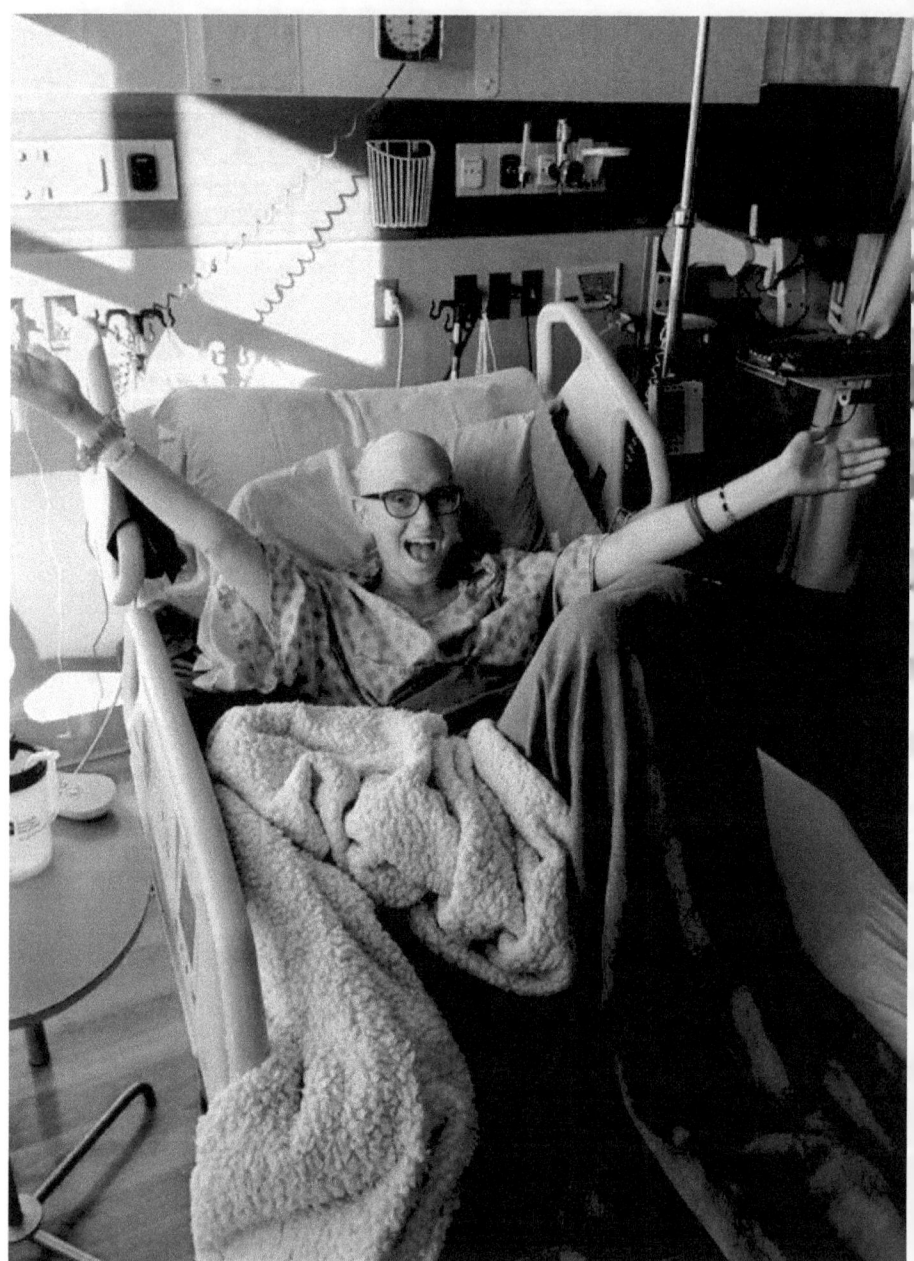

From

Mike and Connie~

Psalm 91:1, 4-5a

Whoever dwells in the shelter of the Most High will rest in the shadow of the Almighty.

He will cover you with His feathers, and under His wings you will find refuge; His faithfulness will be your shield and rampart. You will not fear the terror of night, nor the arrow that flies by day.

"The Bubble" by Connie Washburn.

Living inside the bubble was great. I should know, I used to live there. Happy faces, children's laughter and families having fun. Then one day I was forced outside the bubble. It was the day before Mother's Day. We had a big Saturday planned, packed full of basketball games, paintball and hanging out with friends. That was the morning my 11-year old son suddenly died in my arms from an unexpected heart ailment. That was the day I found myself outside the bubble, looking in.

I wasn't sure how I got there. Everything happened so fast. I found myself staring back in. I was outside the bubble, yet they were all still inside. You know, the happy families were still laughing with their children, enjoying life and making plans for their future. Oh God, No!! I want to be back inside the bubble! I want to hear him laugh again. I frantically searched for a door, a window, any way back inside. Finally, I stopped looking for a way back in and realized I must surrender to my new life outside the bubble.

Life outside the bubble was a place of intense pain. Grief would strike when least expected and drop me to my knees. I was amazed each time I was down the Lord would gently hold out His hand and lift me back up. I had learned so much living on the outside of the bubble. I realized the more I suffered, the more dependent I became on God. The more I learned to trust Him and cling to His promises, the more abundant His faithfulness became. Living outside the bubble had changed me. The things that were once important to me were no longer important. Life seemed to have more meaning and living had more purpose. I was thankful God refined me like gold into the person I had become. There became an urgency in my spirit to be all God wanted me to be. I could hear Him whisper, "I have your little boy and you can trust him to Me. Your time left here is short and you will be reunited with him once again. Now, go, encourage those that hurt, love the unlovable and tell of the things I have done for you." I was reminded that God will take the bad and turn it to good for those who trust in Him.

Then one day a door appeared on the outside of the bubble. The door led back inside. I moved slowly to the door, uncertain about going back inside where people had never touched the deep pain that lingered outside. As I stood at the doorway looking back, I realized I had to make a choice. Stay outside and allow pain to be my constant companion or choose to go inside and use my pain for God's glory. We all have different paths and journeys to walk in this life. I would never have chosen my path to be outside the bubble yet, it was only in those dark hours and the deepest of pain that I began to understand the real meaning of life. There were many more hurting people inside and outside the bubble. I longed to walk beside them and encourage them. I knew the deeper the pain, the deeper the opportunity. I whispered to God, "You have remained faithful to me in my darkest hours, now, I will be faithful and trust You as I open the door and walk in. To God be the glory!

Soren Heart

By Missy Dahlstrom,
Her Mother
Poems by Nathan Dahlstrom,
Her Father

Kiss Me Through
the Fence

*Life can only be understood backwards; but it must
be lived forwards.*
— *Soren Kierkegaard*

I hate this. I don't want to write about it or be on the list. I am angry and broken and I always will be.

The gaping hole can be bandaged, covered up, even ignored for moments, but it is always there. I will live with this for the rest of my earthly life. It is a part of me now.

I'm only writing this because I know there is another mother out there like me who wants to die this morning. Who is hurting so badly, over and over, breathlessly crying on the floor and wanting to crawl down into the grave and die next to her child.

I don't have any good advice. I'm not a professional. I can only tell you what happened to us, and what we did. I know how to bleed. By my wounds...

Rachel

A voice is heard in Ramah,
Lamentation and bitter weeping.
Rachel is weeping for her children;
She refuses to be comforted
for her children because they are no more. - Jeremiah 31:15

Have you ever heard a mother's terrored wail
crying out for her lost child?
No restraint or comfort to her lament—
shattered pieces on the floor,

Have you listened to her weep
from that unseen place—
cut off from her portion,
time stops and
she leaves us.
Heart and breasts and womb still connected,
the love organs in regression
feeling cold and cursed and foreign,
detachment's torture separating flesh from flesh,
the primal space in her unable to be shut off.
There is no mind, no cognizance,
only a heart now—
hemorrhaging in heavy sobs,
trying to bleed itself to death—

and failing,
There is nothing like it.
There is nothing for it.
I hope you never hear it.
It changes you.

My firstborn, Soren, my precious flesh-of-my-flesh, my daughter, left us twelve days after her ninth birthday. An avoidable hunting incident while with my father-in-law saw her whisked away to heaven.

{tears}

{breathe}

It felt like a masterpiece of destruction. The next morning, my three daughters and infant son and I were to fly to New York to meet my husband, Nathan, where he took a new job at a boys' ranch. Our life was forever changed. Four hours before the accident, I had met with our realtor to sign papers to sell our home. In the days following we were left with no car, job, or home.

I remember walking the halls of the hospital afterwards being in disbelief that my heart continued to beat, and my legs could still walk. I felt at any moment my heart would surely stop; there was just no way my body would keep living with this pain. How could I possibly live without her? How could I live with the images I had seen?

We were offered a place to live, out in the middle of nowhere in a little bunkhouse. The house was on a large ranch our friends owned in the Texas panhandle. It was a refuge in the physical sense, but not from any of the pain. We had two little girls (six- & three-years-old) and an infant son (four months) who still needed us. I was nursing Jack, and sometimes it felt like that was the only driving reason for me to continue to eat or drink, so I could keep him alive. The girls had witnessed the tragedy and had their own grief and trauma to work out. When we got settled in a rented house eight weeks later, we bought a king-sized bed so we could all sleep together.

I was sitting on the porch of the bunkhouse when the most beautiful monarch butterfly came and landed on my cheek. I felt as though somehow either God, or my daughter was speaking to me. It was a holy moment. She's still here, I thought for the first time, it's just different now. People don't die. Their caterpillar bodies shrivel up, but they change into something that is miraculous. The butterfly gave me hope.

There were many days when I had to literally tell myself to breathe: Take a breath, Missy. My mind was in such a panic that I had a baby missing. You never really get to rest from that thought. Over and over my mind replayed the problem, and yet all I could do was sit there. Your impulses and adrenaline ready you to fight to the death to save your kid, but there's nothing to do.

Nathan and I made a rule that there was nothing we couldn't say in our grief, as ugly or as hard it might be, nothing was off limits. There was a lot of screaming and cursing and yelling. Breathless rage and sorrow.

The girls could ask any questions or say anything as well. We let it all out, as many times as were necessary.

I learned to move into my grief, to take it along with me. It wasn't going to disappear. I had a choice: I was going to let this destroy me, or I would somehow find a way to survive. I wanted to survive for my family, and I wanted to see my daughter again.

Nathan started writing poems that came out of our madness. They helped us. We would read them together and cry and yell and let the blood flow. Here are a few of them, which tell how it was.

Womanly Things

Livy and Momma sat on the back yard porch
in wood rocking chairs
embroidering, mostly gentle remembrances.
Livy didn't look up from the needle
when she spoke,
'Momma, why don't you wear make-up anymore?
I mean, I know why,
but some days I don't see you cry,
so why don't you wear it then?'
They rocked and they sowed
and kept their eyes on their work,
holiness traveling between
a mother and daughter
about womanly things,
like it has been since Eve.

'Yes, Livy I do cry every day.'
'You mean when I am at school?'
'Yes, Daddy and I cry together most days.
And make-up and tears don't go together very well,
day after day,
tear after tear.
It makes your eyes hurt
and it gets all gummy
and runs.'
'Oh,' Livy said.
'But even if I didn't cry,
I am in mourning for my Sosie,
and my face is a reflection of my heart.
And I don't want to put any colored paint on it.
I hurt so bad...every day...darling,

and I have to let it run its course.'

Livy stopped her little fingers and their sewing in and out
and looked at her mother in the rocker,
a green cotton skirt loose around her waist
fluffed up in her mother's lap holding the crumpled fabric
and all the other sewing necessaries
and her brown hair – gray streaked and dyed now,
tied up in a bun.
A blue scallop shell from the coast
tied on with braided hemp,
a memoir of happier times,
was her only adornment
which they all wore now,
but hers draped around her lovely feminine neck,
blending into a face that had known almost a year
of no make-up
and daily, hourly
devotions of tears.
Tears that left marks like a dry river bed
embedded into the soil and shadow and nuance of her face,
her sad eyes,
pining over the loss of a daughter,
the loss of her god,
and every other loss
wrapped up in an heirloom quilt of her life
in which she sat and walked about in each day.
Courageous and proud in grief,
broken and quiet in everything else.

And the seven-year-old girl said to her Momma,
'Momma,

you're still pretty without make-up,'
and they both went back to their embroidery.
Livy's piece a was a big red heart now,
stitched onto a soft cotton print of little yellow flowers.

Everything we did for the first time was painful. Nothing was missed. Every small routine or anniversary blared at us from a distance like a warning sign for a washed-out bridge. The first bath for the girls without her, the first ride in our family suburban, the first trip to the grocery store passing up all the foods she loved. There were things and places we just couldn't do. Restaurants that had too many memories just hurt too much to go back to. Church - how could we sit in the same pew without her? *How can we sing the songs of the Lord in a foreign land?* It felt like we had to reinvent everything about our family.

Cutting Carrots

I watched you crying,
cutting carrots.
Cooking dinner
for the first time
without your daughter—
helping, asking, talking—
Cheerful Helper
in the kitchen.

I left you alone,
this time,
to do your job
as mother
and as homemaker
and felt your tremor

as you ladled up plates
minus one.

C.S. Lewis wrote, "Her absence is like the sky, spread over everything." There was nothing our grief and pain left untouched. Everything was a painful reminder of what we had lost.

The Hinge

Everything for them
became before and after,
no day was left untouched,
time marked at zero,

~

    rewritten on the hinge
    of the passing of a child
    in the year of their Loss,
    all that was changed was all.

I was able to talk about my anger towards my father-in-law with my husband and a few close friends. And even to him. I knew I wanted to keep the family intact, mainly for the sake of my children, but I had to work through my anger and hurt. I couldn't just pretend. I remember one time when Nathan was at their house, he said, "If you can't go inside their house, then I won't either." He offered to buy me dinner plates, just to break. He bought a punching bag. It was ok to be angry.

Me to You

If you must take that darkened road
that twists so far from sight,
then let me tie a rope from me to you,

95

so wherever you go I may also be
and whoever falls into the pit,
one will feel the tug
and pull the other free.

But if the pit should take us both,
that is rather—
how I would have wanted it.

I was angry at God. I yelled and screamed at him many times
alone in my car. I was living out every mother's worst nightmare.
It takes so much bravery to face the cruelty of those moments. It
is cruel, over and over again.

The only way I understand it, is to acknowledge that I will
never understand it. Parents are not designed to 'accept' this or
'move on' or any other psychobabble. We are designed to die first,
giving our life for a child.

That's why we always say that this is the one true sadness. This
is the only thing that is not natural. We cannot understand it.

I will never be OK with what happened.

I reject it. I reject this fallen world.

The One True Sadness

The one true sadness
In either life
Is when a parent loses their child,
Because it is not natural,
Everything else
Is sentimentality.

Most of my friends listened well. Never judged me. They
walked a very dark path with me. They helped take care of my

family, made sure we had food and groceries, and took care of the kids when we needed help. I don't think I could have survived without my friends. Job 2:13 says, "Then they sat on the ground with him for seven days and seven nights. No one said a word to Job, for they saw that his suffering was too great for words."

The friends that did that; they welded their souls to mine forever. Nothing could separate me from them. It changed them, too, getting that close to our trauma. No one in their right mind wants to hang out with crazy people.

Sitting Shiva

Sit with me-
Watch me tear a hole
Over my heart.

Sit with me-
See that my body and face
I leave unwashed.

Sit with me-
Wear your dark clothes
To honor my dead.

Sit with me-
Invite me not
To parties and feasting.

Sit with me-
As long as it takes
To pass this sorrow.

We learned to plant bluebonnets and wait for their miracle to open every spring. Planting beauty sows hope, and sometimes that is all you have to run on. We need reminders of redemption and resurrection.

Lament for a Bluebonnet

You are the first
To stretch for light,
Your color burst
In March
With none so bright.

And yet, by May
Your glory spirit
Is in decay—
Too short
Your life to covet.

First to live,
First to die,
A law unfairly captive,
Beauty's fate—
A poor time to say goodbye.

But I will always remember
Your delicate, perfect petal
And await your next bloom
When it's cold and frozen
In December.

Finally, perhaps, we came to feel that we had been chosen for this sorrow. I still don't understand why. I still hate it.

But I do believe it's what we do with it that matters now. I want my daughter to be proud of me when I see her again. I don't want our family story to be one of destruction.

Beauty from ashes.

I believe in that promise. I am Israel wrestling with God; I will wrestle with Him until He blesses me. The ashes we carry are a part of us; in our home and on our skin. We carry them because we know someday they will be exchanged for something much better.

Some Lives

Some lives are selected for a great sadness,
Which is a hard selection to take,
The only redemption to find,
Is that a greater love does precede
And to the sadness bind.

And honestly, there's too much to write down, to really tell. Even writing this feels wrong. It's like looking at the cover of a book and acting like you know what's inside. It's like all the cheap articles written by grief counselors titled "What To Say To Grieving People." The only way to really understand, is to go through it. And you wouldn't wish that on your worst enemy.

Grief is complicated. There are new layers and twists and turns constantly revealing themselves to me. Even after thirteen years, I can still be struck with a new layer of grief. I've learned to allow myself to fully feel those new griefs, and old ones that creep up. Sit with it. Grief must be dealt with and cannot be ignored.

I have also learned that I can set my grief aside. I cannot live 24 hours consumed in it. By setting it aside, I am not setting my love aside for my daughter, as I once thought. My grief is not *her*.

It feels cheapened by writing this to strangers because grief is an *intimacy*. In some ways, it's like sex, it only works right between two people alone. To truly partake in grief is to stand naked before another, before God, and watch your soul be rendered. You are completely undone. How do you do that in a book, without it just being a freak-show to be ogled by those passing by? To be a sermon anecdote used to increase the pathos on Sunday morning from 9-10 o'clock.

Generally, with actual I-want-to-die-from-this-pain grief, we cover our eyes and move past it.

Death Now

They pulled a plastic green
fake-grass turf over the dirt pile
that sat next to the hole
where a casket hovered in limbo
while the preacher preached
of joy and happiness above
and a stingless death below
without making eye contact
or letting silence speak
and someone whispered
"they're trying to stay positive"
and "best not to dwell on it"
and "best to get back to work"
and no one wore black
and no one really noticed
and no one stayed after
to shovel the dirt pile that
they had pulled a plastic green
fake-grass turf over.

In that intimacy God is meeting with us. Job survived being singled out by God for destruction by believing "YHWH gives and takes away." He knew YHWH through both sides of his identity—a giver and taker. In both actions, God was trying to meet with him. Sad is not wrong. It is not faithless. It is an opening to half of the truth of God. You must receive it.

"Why have you forsaken me?" is NOT a scripture cue from Psalm 22 from the wise and unfeeling Christ to comfort his friends. It is the peak of his humanity screaming at God, saying, "Hey, you're not who I thought you were!!! I don't get this!!!"

If our precious Christ can scream and wonder, and even challenge, I don't think God hates us for doing so.

We want our kids with us. We want to die before they do. To fade away, looking up into their strong eyes and feeling like we did our part. To feel their young hands in our old ones and know they have tools to navigate the trials of life, to pass it on. No fear, no sadness at the end. Just perhaps, peace. That's not so bad, is it?

We lost that. And the longing goes on and on at the broken seam in our life story. Nothing swallows it up and takes it away.

Perhaps only that we endure.

And love. The little passport in our hand that we know will cross over and tie us together. Nobody gets to take that away.

So, finally, I survive, because love and beauty exist. Sometimes the beauty is easy to see, other times we must search to find it, but it is there. The beauty we experience becomes my down payment that everything God promised is true, no matter how much sorrow we must endure here. I cannot deny that beauty exists, and that it proves God left it for us in this cursed time of struggle and misery.

And one glorious day, all will be restored, and I will get all my years without my daughter back.

Grief's Evanescence

One little lifetime
is not too much,
to love a daughter
I can't touch.

There will be no
grief's evanescence,
the healing hands of time
heal not sorrow's nuance.

I will not box you up
as an ethic worth chasing,
and act as if moving on
be a moral worth faking.

I will love you in your absence,
a buoyant vigil between the shores,
waiting – watching for the morn
when riven heart restores.

I will love you every day,
all the days I have breath,
so when I see you again
we'll prove love floats over death.

There is a fence between us now, but that is all. A fence. And sometimes, sometimes it doesn't feel so separating. When butterflies land on my face in fields of bluebonnets, I can just about feel her.

Kiss Me Through the Fence

I dropped you off at your school
One perfect September day
You ran to the playground
No kiss for Daddy -
Too busy for play
I watched ponytails bounce along
And wept inside my chest
But as I turned to go
You hollered from the fence.

Daddy come here close
I have something for you
You almost slipped away
Before I said I love you
I'll see you soon
School is just a bit
It's only a couple hours
Bend down low
And kiss me through the fence.

Little girl
You went away too soon
So late at night
I always think about you
And I think it's possible
If we both try
You on one side
And me here tonight
Hold my heart for one second
And kiss me through the fence.

103

Daddy come here close
I have something for you
You almost slipped away
Before I said I love you
I'll see you soon
School is just a bit
It's only a couple hours
Bend down low
And kiss me through the fence.

Appendix
Two Sonnets

Love Sonnet #11

I stuck my nose in your pink Nikes,
To get a whiff of you,
Before I sped off to work,
So far away I flew,

I wear your necklace every day,
A tiny Texas flag charm,
We bought in San Antonio,
On a day when all was warm.

Because I still need to love you,
In more than memories,
I need to touch your scent,
And be where you are sensory.

Love cannot stop, in the blinking of an eye,
It goes on and grows, it never says goodbye.

Love Sonnet #15

I can smell you sure
when I passing think
of your cherry swimsuit,
the sun your pale skin pinked.

Grass and water and a dog
with little feet that squish,
so on this 15th birthday
that is what I most wish.

To hold your bony knees,
to brush your sopping hair,
to wet kiss your forehead,
to sit on the porch and stare.

A blond-haired girl, and all my hopes juxtapose,
with the scent of light and love and a water hose.

From

Mike and Connie~

Hebrews 4:16

*Let us then approach God's throne of grace with
confidence, so that we may receive mercy and find
grace to help us in our time of need.*

When the "why's" remain unanswered, and the pain feels
unbearable, we are still given the assurance that God will
strengthen us. He will carry us through the weight of our grief,
offering us mercy and grace every step of the way. Even in our
deepest moments of heartache, He is faithful to provide the
strength we need to endure, and His love will guide us through the
hardest times. Though we may never fully understand our loss,
we can trust that He will be our source of comfort and support,
helping us navigate the overwhelming pain with His presence and
compassion.

Brandon

By Brett Menke,
His Father

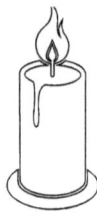

Brandon was the oldest of my three boys. Brandon and Alex are my children from a previous marriage. My youngest son, Elliott, was adopted in 2009. Brandon almost always had a different way of seeing things than most, and was generous to a fault. Brandon would do without in order to help someone else. While he displayed some selfless qualities at times, he also fought some enormous personal battles, the most taxing of which was drug use. The drugs were always there during ebbs and flows, eventually robbing him of who he really was. They also ushered in a series of events that would leave Brandon feeling as if there was no reason to live.

When Brandon died, he was just days away from his 39th birthday, but I most often remember him as a young boy around ages of eight to twelve. I remember him playing trumpet in the band, doing science projects, fishing at his grandpa's pond, and playing baseball games. Perhaps I remember him that way to block out the negative and replace it with the innocent times, the times when we were closer, the times when we were a family.

Brandon professed his faith as a teenager, but it seems that he never fully grasped his position in Christ. As he grew up, I struggled with the fact that he went down a darker path. There were some warning signs at home that I should have paid more attention to. It was a strange feeling when I first opened the garage door and saw Brandon with his nose buried in the gas tank of his ATV. No one prepares you as a parent for those hard things.

In 2000, I moved to Fort Worth, Texas, with my two sons and my then-wife, Allison. In November 2001, both my sons moved back to Arkansas to live with their mother. It was a tough season, and I'm sure it was hard on everyone involved.

For many years, Brandon was struggling with drug use, which caused distance between us. We hardly met or talked, even when we visited Arkansas. Communicating with him was challenging due to his incoherent speech and tendency to repeat himself, often leading to rants. However, in the spring of 2021, my prayers for Brandon seemed to have been answered when he ended up in jail. This event led him to join a Christian program that helps reform addicts, and for a while, it seemed like he was making progress. The Lord works in mysterious ways indeed.

Several months had passed when I received the news that Brandon had left the facility and exited the program. My hopes were short-lived, but by summer, the Lord had orchestrated a meeting between Brandon and a man who was a follower of Christ. This man not only gave Brandon a job but also shared the love of Christ with him. It wasn't long before Brandon told me how God had rescued and transformed him. He shared story after story about how God's protective hand was on him and brought him to meet his boss, who genuinely showed him what grace looked like. I was so encouraged and hopeful to visit him soon.

In late June or early July, Brandon mentioned that he would be working with his boss about an hour and forty-five minutes from where I lived, so we planned a visit. On Friday, July 2nd, 2021, I saw my son in person for the last few hours I would ever get to see him. Our time was special as Brandon's speech was normal, and his conversation was coherent. Brandon once again shared how God's mercy spared him, and he considered it no coincidence. Brandon praised the Lord for his mercy and protection even when he had run from him. Brandon even shared how much he wanted to be a good father to his three children. After our visit, I returned home with a genuine belief that the prodigal son had finally come home. In the following months, Brandon and I kept in touch by phone and text with relative frequency, but then things began to taper off, and I began to grow concerned.

On April 22nd, 2022, I received the last text message from Brandon I would ever receive.

On Thursday around 11 pm, my then-wife, Allison, entered my room and handed me her phone. On the line was my middle son, Alex. It was the type of call you know the moment you answer, your world will never be the same. In agony, Alex explained that his brother was dead and that he had taken his own life. I don't remember much of the conversation after that. Initially, there was only shock, and my mind was completely numb. I remember just sitting on the bed, sobbing. There were more phone calls from Alex and Brandon's mother, and gradually, details began to come out.

Before I retell the last few hours of Brandon's life, I need to frame up the events leading up to his decision to end his life. As I mentioned earlier, our communication had dwindled. I had wondered if Brandon had fallen back into drug use, and unfortunately, he had. While he was in jail, his girlfriend and the mother of his three children chose to abandon the relationship. Brandon was working two jobs, but being back on drugs led to his losing the work he had.

The story becomes clearer as we follow his downward spiral. He lost his girlfriend, children, and income, developed a drug habit, and fell behind on his support. I have heard that a person with a habit will justify their use over anything else in their life, and I am sure by this time, Satan had Brandon on the ropes. I imagine the evil one whispering in his ear, reminding him of his failures, telling him he is worthless, that God doesn't care, or that he would make it all go away. Telling him that he is all alone, that nobody cares about him. The serpent is crafty and has had a long time honing his skills as he looks for someone to devour. Sadly, Satan knew exactly what it would take to send Brandon over the edge.

The day Brandon took his life, he had spent the night in his pickup truck. I am not entirely clear on why, but for some reason, Brandon left the place where he was staying that afternoon. He took a backpack and a shotgun with him and set out on foot. At some point, someone spotted him walking along the road with the firearm on his back and was concerned enough to call the police to report a potentially dangerous person. I have replayed this scene over and over in my mind many times, imagining what I would have done had I been in their shoes, and I would have made the same call. However, I still cannot comprehend what might have been going through Brandon's mind.

Grief has been no stranger in my life. I have lost family and friends, including my father and mother. My brother was killed by a drunk driver when he was 40 years old. I have endured the loss of a stillborn child. I have suffered the heartbreak of divorce more than once. But by far, Brandon's suicide has been the most grievous. No words can accurately describe the trauma, raising its head at the most inopportune times and with no apparent trigger. I don't have to hear a song, see a picture, or relive a memory. Sometimes, the grief just shows up and crushes you like a freight train.

For instance, in the days following Brandon's death, I was grilling on the back patio as I often do in the summer. For whatever reason, I was suddenly so overwhelmed that tears streamed down my face. There was no trigger at all, no mental pictures, nothing; it just showed up and left almost as quickly as it came. For me, the biggest obstacle has been not knowing when or where grief will strike—not knowing the duration or if you will be overcome in the produce aisle at the grocery store surrounded by total strangers. The feeling that this certainty will never fully relent is something I must entrust to God.

During this season, my wife and I lived separately in the same house. Ultimately, in 2023, our marriage ended in divorce. We had been married just days shy of 31 years. I was staying in one of the spare bedrooms, and it was there where I took the phone call about Brandon's death.

Life's storms came at full gale and respected nothing. I still had to earn a living and be a dad to my youngest son. After the divorce, I had to deal with being separated from everything I had known for all those years. But I still had to carry on, and nothing bowed as a courtesy to my loss or grief. Thankfully, the God of the universe, Jehovah-Rapha, our great Healer, meets me every morning and carries me throughout the day. The Lord is my strength. While I still experience grief, it is only by the grace of God and his mercy that I can function. There are days when I get up for work and have zero ambition. On those days, my time with God in the morning is the lifeline for the day. When everything else is stripped away, God is truly all we need.

When I think of the times grief has struck since Brandon's death, I immediately remember that with the grief, there was also God's mercy. Most often, when the pain comes, God doesn't allow me to stay there long. He pulls me out, not allowing me to sink into self-pity. He reminds me I am his. I can't ask for a better friend. Thank you, Jesus!

Looking back, I realize that God was working in everything to prepare me to walk out my earthly journey and ultimately truly surrender to Him. Isaiah 55:8 says, "For my thoughts are not your thoughts, neither are your ways my ways, declares the Lord." This Scripture has been more true than ever, especially during this trial. When I needed encouragement, it came from those who you would expect to be there and from some who were very unlikely.

My cousin Lou was one of the likely ones. He and I have been close since childhood, I guess because our fathers and mothers were so close. We are "double cousins." I'm not sure that is an actual thing, but that is what we always called ourselves growing up. My mother's sister married my dad's brother; this constantly tethered us together with a special bond. We all lived in Berkley, Missouri, a suburb of St. Louis. Frequently, our family would go to Uncle Rich and Aunt Joyce's house, and they would often return the favor. Lou has always been a spiritual guide for me as well. He is as straight an arrow as I know, and his love for Christ has always been forthright and never hidden. He is a true mentor.

Lou has two biological children and two adopted children. His two boys, Nicholas and Josiah, are his biological children, and his adopted children are Victoria Grace and Kathryn Elizabeth. Lou has also suffered loss. His little son Benjamin passed at five months *in utero*. He lost his youngest son, Josiah, in an automobile accident, and his marriage to his first wife ended in divorce after thirty years. It is remarkable how similar our stories are. God has used Lou as an incredible friend in my life. Since Brandon's death and my recent divorce, Lou has always been there when I needed him, which has been often. Lou is indeed closer to me than a brother. Thank you, Lord, for providing the human support we need!

Oddly enough, an unexpected light in the darkness came from my first wife. In the aftermath of Brandon's death, we communicated by phone as I got information about the arrangements. Since that time, she and I texted somewhat frequently to help manage the grief. Tuesday, August 9th, had been an exceedingly sorrowful day for me. There was no particular reason for it, but it had been nevertheless. I do remember feeling very much alone. Around 6:00 pm that evening, I got a text message from Brandon's mother. that read:

> *"So you've been on my mind a lot. Like I said, I feel I have lots of support, and you don't. I'm burnt out on texts, but I wanted to share this with you. I've been trying hard not to let my mind go to the should of, could of, would of, you know? It did race in my mind tonight but on different tangents. I remember crying and saying out loud, "No, I don't want to do this, I can't." And in that instant, I received God's peace. It washed over me, and I instantly felt calm. Every time someone prays, and they feel like it isn't enough.... It truly is. I was just blessed, and my prayer tonight is that you feel His peace, too."*

So, on an evening when I felt totally alone and was battling grief, my first wife shared with me how God had shown her his peace. Even now, her words lift me when I read them. In a time of unparalleled pain and suffering, God blessed two people with the same act of mercy. What an awesome, loving God!

When I recall the days shortly after Brandon's death, one would think a believer in Jesus would cling to His Word with all their strength. Oddly, that wasn't the case for me. There was a trip to Arkansas to take, so I had to throw together some things and get there as quickly as I could. I did pray a lot during that time, but I wasn't reading His Word. There was, however, a steadiness that only God could provide. Even though I wasn't reading His Word, Scripture did come to mind often, and the Holy Spirit translated my groaning to the Father. The trip went well, and I had a wonderful visit with my middle son, Alex. We got to ride around his grandfather's farm, where I spent a lot of time in days past. Under the circumstances, it was pretty peaceful, and that peace could only have come from the Lord.

However, after that trip, I knew I needed to not let my mind run in the wrong direction. I had battled negative thoughts of "Am I being punished?" "Am I not good enough of a husband to keep a wife?" "Am I less than?" I knew that Satan used Brandon's battle with drugs which ultimately caused his death. Yet, Brandon's last words revealed he was exhausted by the spiritual battle. I knew I had to shore myself back up in the Lord. I had to supplement and bolster my mind with God's Word to get in a better place to do battle in the grief process. God was so faithful as I took one little step towards Him and His Word. He was faithful not to leave me in the pit or abandon me. I realized there truly was a way back! I began to lean into the Scriptures for God's acceptance and strength.

These are some of the Scriptures that have been monumental in strengthening me:

> *Revelation 21:4 – "He will wipe away every tear from their eyes, and death shall be no more, neither shall there be mourning, nor crying, nor pain anymore, for the former things have passed away."*

Psalm 147:3 – "He heals the brokenhearted and binds up their wounds."

Psalm 34:18 – "The Lord is near to the brokenhearted and saves the crushed in spirit."

Matthew 11:28-30 – "Come to me, all who labor and are heavy laden, and I will give you rest. Take my yoke upon you, and learn from me, for I am gentle and lowly in heart, and you will find rest for your souls. For my yoke is easy, and my burden is light."

Romans 8:18 – "For I consider that the sufferings of this present time are not worth comparing with the glory that is to be revealed to us."

I could list dozens of excerpts from God's Word, but I challenge you to dust off that old Bible on the shelf and glean some wisdom. See how God speaks to you through His Word. It will be invaluable throughout your healing journey. As I got into the Word of God, it got into me, then I found myself thinking differently, and my actions followed. I joined a Bible study group and continued to find truth, strength, and solace in His Word while surrounded by a community.

In managing grief from the loss of a child or a loved one, don't be tempted to withdraw. In our fragility, humans are not meant to face pain alone. People grieve differently, but isolation can be counterproductive and dangerous. Of course, there will be times when we need to get alone with God and let Him do what only He can.

A few things have been crucial for me. I have not been naïve enough to think I am too strong to get help from a good counselor. There have been times when I knew I had to talk to a professional to help me sort some things out. Don't let pride or the fear of being labeled "unstable" deter you from seeing a reputable, licensed counselor. Also, don't be tempted to believe that you can manage the grief on your own. Surround yourself with solid, supportive individuals who have been through the storm. It may not be the same storm as yours, but it is a storm nonetheless. We truly do need each other to survive this human experience.

Most importantly, spend time with God. James 4:8a says, *"Draw near to God, and he will draw near to you. If you seek him, you will find him."* Time with Him is the key to healing, so prioritize time with God. I encourage you to meditate on it and claim His Word until you believe it, and I promise His grace will be sufficient for you, too.

> *2 Corinthians 12:9 – "But he said to me, 'My grace is sufficient for you, for my power is made perfect in weakness.' Therefore, I will boast all the more gladly of my weaknesses so that the power of Christ may rest upon me."*

For almost 31 years, I have been in relative comfort—comfort in my career, comfort in my relationship, comfort with family, and, to a degree, comfort with my church life. I gave God the credit for what he has provided, but I don't think I grasped the true meaning of John 15:5: *I am the vine; you are the branches. Whoever abides in me and I in him, it is he that bears much fruit, for apart from me, you can do nothing.*

This season has been the most crushing, paralyzing season I have ever experienced. I lost my mother in February of 2020, my oldest son in August of 2022, and my wife and youngest son in November of 2022 when they moved out of our home. In all my comfort, I didn't realize that God really is in control. The transition to single life has been challenging. Working from my home hasn't helped with isolation either. I know that in all events of our lives, there is a purpose in it. The key is to be tapped into the Vine so much so that we don't fail to see the purpose for what it is.

For me, two things have become glaringly apparent. First, I have come to realize that God is all I truly need. I can't count the times throughout the day that the Holy Spirit asks, "Do you truly trust me?" There have been times when I had to be honest and answer no, not totally. Yet, in all the chaos, this amazing, steadfast strength still carries me through another day. Without a doubt, I know this is from God, and I have nothing to contribute. He makes me strong in my weakness. I have realized that surrendering to God brings peace, but fighting it is exhausting. As I surrendered to God, even though I didn't understand all the pain and loss, I found true peace that carries me through each day.

Secondly, the words you are reading testify that God never wastes any of our hurt, pain, or tears. Grief is bigger and more than we can take, and only God can take us through. We cannot do it ourselves. If we fight trusting God, it can be overwhelming and exhausting. We can get caught in anesthetizing ourselves and stay stuck in grief forever. But there is always a way out with God. There have been many evenings after work when things slow down, and the silence in my home is almost unbearable. In those moments, I have asked the Lord to bring people into my life with whom I can share Brandon's story. I changed my focus and asked God to let me share with them that, as agonizing as our loss is, we don't have to bear the weight on our own. God, in His mercy, will embrace us and comfort us in ways we can't even imagine. In answer to my prayer, God has given me this opportunity to pen some words that hopefully will help others with similar stories.

John 16:33 says, *"I have said these things to you, that in me you may have peace. In the world, you will have tribulation. But take heart; I have overcome the world."*

I pray that you will be comforted, that God will strengthen you in the dark times, and that our great Jehovah-Rapha will heal you and make you whole again as only He can. His love is unfathomable, and I challenge you to believe even when it doesn't make sense. Everyone will walk their grief journey differently, but as you surrender and trust God, you will find He is trustworthy. We are still here with purpose, and I pray that we let God's love define the rest of our stories.

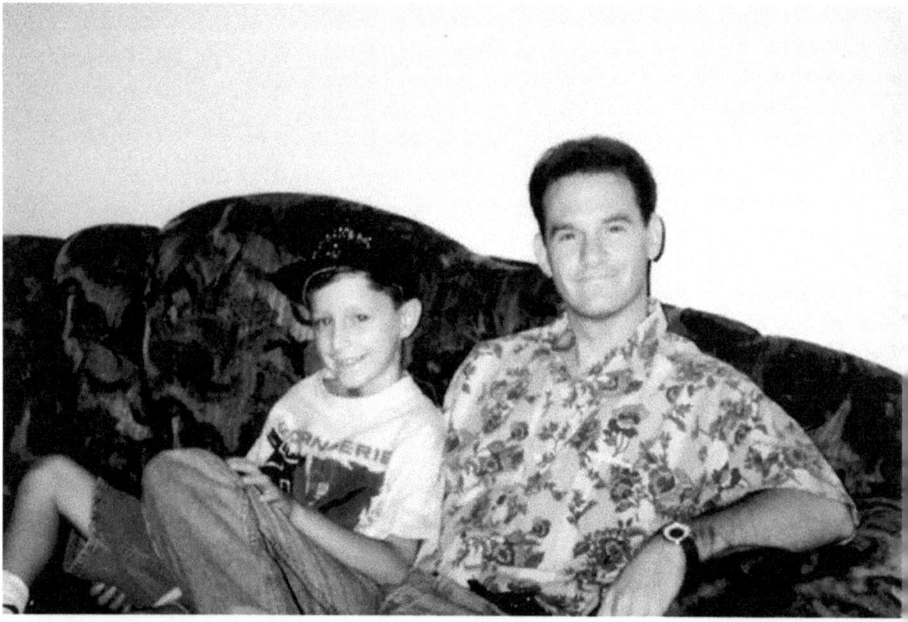

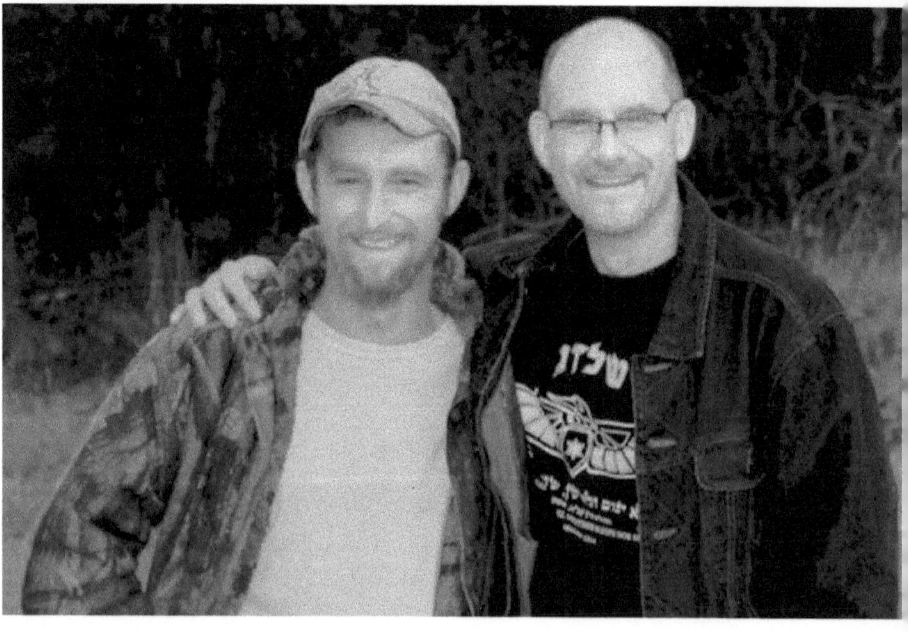

From

Mike and Connie~

Psalm 55:22

Cast your cares on the Lord and He will sustain you;
He will never let the righteous be shaken

Earlier in this Psalm, David expressed a desire to escape the storms that relentlessly pursued him, longing for peace and rest. But God showed him a different path to true rest—one that comes not from running away, but from trusting Him. "Cast your cares on the Lord," David says, "and let Him sustain you." Even in the midst of the fiercest storms, God is our rest. He is the steady anchor when life feels like it's crashing all around us. Our assurance lies in Him, knowing that He will never allow the righteous to be shaken. No matter the depth of our grief, He is always there, holding us, sustaining us, and providing the peace we desperately need.

Jeffrey

By Jeannie L. Williams,
His Mother

✝

On November 28, 2001, my husband Jeff and I sat in the hospital room, cradling our newborn son, contemplating his name. Naming our child was a momentous decision, one we approached with care and meaning. Jeff was adamant that he didn't want a "Junior," but he liked the idea of using his own first name, Jeffrey. We also wanted to incorporate Lee, which was not only Jeff's mother's middle name but also a name with significance in my family. As we discussed and deliberated, the idea that brought a smile to my face was realizing that his initials, JLW, would match mine.

Fast forward to June 7, 2013, a day that started with the anticipation of a trip but ended in unimaginable tragedy. Jeffrey and I embarked on an overnight journey to Boone, NC, to pick up his sister, Breanne, from an anatomy camp. Earlier that day, before setting off, we attended an informational meeting at Chick-fil-A for a new Lego club in town. It was a busy morning, filled with excitement and plans for the day ahead.

Jeffrey, always sociable and friendly, enjoyed catching up with old friends and making new ones at Chick-fil-A. His enthusiasm for the Lego club was infectious, and I couldn't help but marvel at how effortlessly he could connect with others, young and old alike.

After the meeting, we hit the road towards Boone. The drive was scenic, winding through the mountains that surrounded us. Jeffrey and I chatted about his plans for the summer, his excitement palpable as he looked forward to spending time with friends and exploring new hobbies.

Upon reaching Boone, our first order of business was locating our hotel and settling in before picking up Breanne the next morning. I remember driving through the unfamiliar streets, trying to get my bearings while Jeffrey eagerly pointed out landmarks and restaurants he wanted to visit.

By then, it was approaching evening, and Jeffrey and I decided to have dinner at Ruby Tuesday's, a restaurant nearby that he had spotted earlier. Jeffrey loved their salad bar, and I fondly remember watching him carefully select and arrange each ingredient on his plate. It was a simple moment, yet it encapsulated his meticulous nature and love for good food.

We checked into our hotel and were assigned a room on the first floor. However, as soon as we entered, I noticed a distinct smell of cigarette smoke lingering in the air. Concerned for our health, especially Jeffrey's, I inspected the room further and found ashtray residue on the bedside table and the faint aroma of smoke drifting in through a cracked window.

I immediately went to the front desk to request another room. The hotel staff apologized, explaining that they had issues with a repeat guest who disregarded the no-smoking policy. They promptly assigned us to a different room, room 225, which they assured me was smoke-free and cleaned thoroughly.

Jeffrey and I made our way to room 225 around 8:30 PM, or thereabouts. It had been a long day of driving and running errands, but we were finally settled in for the night. I suggested we hit the pool for a swim before bedtime, but Jeffrey suddenly realized he had forgotten to pack his bathing suit. It was a teachable moment for me as a mom, learning to let him take more responsibility. Instead of getting upset, Jeffrey opted for a quick shower, looking forward to some screen time on his iPad afterwards. I called Jeff to let him know we were in the room and would call him after picking up Breanne.

Meanwhile, I turned on the Weather Channel to check the forecast. Storms were predicted in the area, adding a touch of unease to the evening. I plugged in my phone by the bedside, preparing for the night ahead.

After his shower, Jeffrey settled comfortably on the bed, immersed in a game on his iPad. I smiled at the sight, grateful for these simple moments together. Little did I know it would be my last vision of him like that.

Feeling a bit worn out myself, I decided to freshen up before calling it a night. I went into the bathroom to remove my contacts and wash my face. But as I stood at the sink, a wave of nausea swept over me, followed by a sharp upset in my stomach. I quickly closed the bathroom door and sat down on the toilet, hoping the discomfort would pass.

The layout of the room was unusual. Unlike most hotel rooms, I couldn't see the bed from the bathroom door, emphasizing its spaciousness. And because of the size of the room, I remember thinking Jeffrey may not be able to hear me. As I sat on the bathroom toilet, dizziness overcame me, and I feared I might collapse. My mind raced with worry—how would I get help? My phone lay by the bed, just out of reach. Thoughts of Jeffrey flashed through my head. Who would take care of him if I had to go to the hospital? Who would pick up Breanne from camp?

On Sunday, June 9th, the room was filled with the steady hum of monitors and the murmur of voices. Slowly, my eyes fluttered open to see Jeff and Breanne standing beside me. I tried to make sense of the clock on the wall, but the hospital's logo distorted the time, and without my contacts, everything was a blur. I couldn't speak, so I attempted to gesture toward my wrist, desperate to know the time. It struck me as curious—why was I fixated on the time in such a moment? The confusion lingered, clouding my thoughts as I struggled to comprehend what had happened.

After what felt like an eternity of uncertainty, Jeff finally handed me a pen and paper. With trembling hands, I began to write, forming the letter "J." Jeff, understanding immediately, gently took my hand in his and looked deeply into my eyes. "Jeffrey is with Jesus," he said softly. The words pierced through me, leaving me speechless and numb. I tried to voice my questions, mouthing "what" and "why" over and over again, but no sound emerged. The weight of grief and confusion was overwhelming.

As the hours passed, my mind raced with fragments of memories and unanswered questions. I caught glimpses of Breanne, reminding me that we had picked her up from camp. But the details were hazy—did Jeffrey and I visit a school lab where we might have been exposed to something harmful? The uncertainty gnawed at me, leaving me grasping for answers that no one seemed able to provide.

Later that day, a friend entered the room, and in my attempt to communicate, I pointed upwards, trying to convey that Jeffrey was now with Jesus. My words failed me, but my friend initially misunderstood, thinking I was professing my love for Jesus.

Eventually, he grasped the truth. The news of Jeffrey's passing had already spread, though the cause remained a mystery. I had been in the hospital for more than 24 hours by then, grappling with the sudden loss and the haunting questions that plagued my thoughts.

The next morning, Jeff gently informed me that we would be leaving the hospital to go back to Rock Hill. He explained that Jeffrey was also being moved, and he wanted us to leave simultaneously. I was transferred by ambulance. They escorted us through a back entrance, where a security guard stood watch outside my door later that day. Despite the unusual attention, my thoughts were surprisingly calm. I realized I needed to trust the caregivers around me and allow myself to rest. I didn't comprehend the reason for the media attention, but I knew it was there. Still grappling with unanswered questions about what had happened to Jeffrey and me, I awaited clarity. When the first doctor entered my hospital room and mentioned carbon monoxide poisoning, I felt a surge of surprise. Immediately, Jeff and another hospital staff member took the doctor outside my room. I thought it was odd, but I remember a supernatural sense of "rest and trust."

The days that followed blurred together as I underwent blood transfusions, various tests, and focused on rebuilding my physical strength. Throughout it all, the hospital staff showed incredible kindness, even accommodating my 17-year-old daughter in a nearby room so she could rest and spend time with friends and family. Despite her young age, Breanne became a pillar of support, ensuring everyone followed through with their promises. Alongside a dear friend, she even took on the task of finding a dress for me for Jeffrey's memorial service, a thoughtful gesture that touched my heart deeply.

Upon my release from the hospital on Saturday, we made our way to the funeral home to see Jeffrey. Entering that room, where my beloved son lay in repose, was a moment etched forever in my heart. It's incredibly difficult to articulate the emotions that surged through me as I stood there, staring at Jeffrey's still form in the casket. Jeff had seen him earlier in Boone, confirming his identity. Jeffrey wore the outfit we had carefully chosen—his shirt neatly pressed, pants crisply folded, and his bangs gently brushed over his forehead. Tears streamed down my cheeks uncontrollably, and my heart ached with a profound sense of loss. Seeing him lying there, so peaceful yet so lifeless, was a surreal and heartbreaking experience.

Jeffrey's memorial service was a poignant testament to the love and impact he had on everyone who knew him. Jeff, along with our pastor and music minister from Northside Baptist, took charge of planning the service. They decided to wait until Father's Day, which, although difficult, was a fitting tribute to Jeff as a father mourning the loss of his beloved son. Recognizing that Northside Baptist wouldn't accommodate the expected turnout, First Baptist Church of Rock Hill graciously opened their doors for the service.

Before the main service, we gathered for a private graveside service. I was wheeled out to the center of the cemetery, surrounded by our close-knit circle of family and friends. The sight of beautiful roses adorning Jeffrey's casket brought both beauty and sadness.

Stepping into the sanctuary for the main service, I was overwhelmed by the outpouring of love and support. As we entered, everyone rose to their feet, a powerful testament to the impact Jeffrey had on our community. I recall marveling at the number of attendees, some standing at the back of the room, and a sense that even the balcony was filled with mourners. Later, it struck me as odd, realizing that the church auditorium actually had no balcony—a detail I had overlooked in the midst of my grief.

The service itself was a moving tribute filled with special moments and heartfelt testimonies. The Gospel was shared, highlighting Jeffrey's short but impactful life. It was a day marked by tears and laughter, sorrow and celebration, as we remembered and honored Jeffrey's legacy in our lives.

A few days after Jeffrey's memorial service, Jeff sat me down to share more details about what had transpired on that tragic night. It was revealed that carbon monoxide had leaked into our room from a faulty pool heater. Shockingly, we learned that just seven weeks prior, two other people had tragically passed away in that very same room due to the same issue.

The revelation added a chilling layer of sorrow to our already overwhelming grief. Knowing that others had suffered a similar fate in that room made us question how such a tragedy could occur more than once. It underscored the severity and magnitude of the situationand left us grappling with the harsh reality of what had happened to our dear Jeffrey.

The guilt I felt was immense. Why did Jeffrey die and not me? I wrestled endlessly with this question. They said the carbon monoxide poisoning was stronger where Jeffrey was, less in the bathroom where I sat with the door closed, the light and fan on. But that explanation, while it offered some clarity, didn't ease the burden of guilt that weighed on my heart.

People often offered comforting clichés: "God's not finished with you yet" or "It just wasn't your time." But those platitudes didn't resonate with me. They didn't provide the solace I desperately sought in the wake of such a profound loss. The truth was, I might never in this lifetime understand why this happened. And when I reach heaven, perhaps I won't even want to know anymore.

I'd always disliked the saying "everything happens for a reason." Things happened, period. Life is messy and unpredictable. Sometimes tragedies occur without rhyme or reason. Yet society often pressures us to find meaning or justification in every traumatic event, as if knowing the reason would make it all easier to bear.

In moments of despair, I reminded myself that God held our days in His hands. I clung to the hope that in trusting Him and finding rest in His love, I could begin to heal from this unimaginable loss. God knows our days on this earth; I knew I had to trust and rest.

Establishing a foundation in Jeffrey's name initially felt urgent. We launched a nonprofit to raise awareness and support others, and for seven years it did meaningful work. Yet, personally, I struggled to find a lasting sense of purpose in it. Discussing Jeffrey's death at events aimed at raising awareness often left me feeling drained rather than empowered.

Eventually, we shifted our support to The Jenkins Foundation, which focuses on advocating for improved coding for carbon monoxide alarms in hotels and commercial spaces, and educating the public about this silent danger. Redirecting our efforts to support their cause felt more aligned with our journey, and allowed us to contribute to a cause that resonated deeply with our experience.

About eleven months after Jeffrey passed away, I met a mom whose son had been gone for as many years as he had been alive. He was fifteen when he died, and she was approaching what she called his "heaven date" rather than an anniversary. I remember looking at her and thinking, "She's still standing." Despite her immense loss, she had found purpose in doing incredible work for other children. It made me reflect deeply because, honestly, I hadn't found that same clarity of purpose. I'm still learning to live each day in a way that glorifies God and perhaps serves as a testimony to other moms who face the unthinkable loss of a child.

It's not easy. People say things meant to be comforting but end up being more hurtful because they don't truly understand the depth of this pain. Yet, through it all, I hold on to hope; the hope that I will see Jeffrey again one day. It's a hope that keeps me going, even on the hardest days. And I'm reminded daily that Jesus is the reason for that hope, as Romans 8:24-25 says, "For in this hope we were saved. But hope that is seen is no hope at all. Who hopes for what they already have? But if we hope for what we do not yet have, we wait for it patiently."

Romans 15:13 also brings me comfort: "May the God of hope fill you with all joy and peace as you trust in him, so that you may overflow with hope by the power of the Holy Spirit."

Greg Laurie once wrote, "It's not easy to believe in the goodness and glory of God when your heart is breaking. But when you do, when you rest your full faith and confidence in God— even when nothing else on earth seems to make sense—you will never be the loser... in this life, or the next." These words resonate deeply with me, reminding me that even in the midst of pain and confusion, trusting in God's goodness brings a peace that surpasses understanding.

Going Forward

In the months and years following Jeffrey's passing, navigating through the difficult aftermath of carbon monoxide poisoning was a journey marked by God's grace and the unwavering support of loved ones.

When I think back to those initial days in the hospital, everything seems like a blur. There were security guards stationed outside my room, shielding me from the distressing news reports. My husband, Jeff, was my rock through it all. He took on the role of protector, filtering information and patiently explaining what had happened when I was ready to hear it. His presence was a true, unexplainable blessing during those early, fragile days.

Reflecting on the ordeal, I can't help but attribute my ability to remain calm and avoid anxiety (so that my body could heal) to the Holy Spirit's guidance. It was God's grace that sustained me through the neurological challenges caused by the poisoning. I've come to realize that everyone's experience with carbon monoxide poisoning is unique. Despite the lingering effects, I am grateful that I can still live independently and function normally.

Being a mom to Breanne after Jeffrey's passing was a challenge that God helped me navigate. Breanne's decision to attend a local private Christian school brought relief during a time when homeschooling (which I had previously done) would have been overwhelming. The school community embraced her, offering support and a sense of normalcy that allowed me the space to process my grief and heal physically. Their kindness, from teachers to counselors, lifted a significant weight off my shoulders and gave me more comfort that Breanne had a safe space to share her grief when she tried to protect me from it.

Breanne's steadfast faith was a pillar of strength. At Jeffrey's viewing, she reminded me that his body was just a vessel and that his soul was with Jesus. Her unwavering belief in God's plan, even amid tragedy, was a source of encouragement for me. She amazes me.

Months later, facing a cancer diagnosis and surgery added another layer of challenge. With neuropathy preventing me from undergoing traditional intravenous chemotherapy, I turned to oral chemo. Through it all, my faith and dependence on God grew stronger. His peace continued to sustain me, even as legal matters loomed and the question of accountability arose. It's amazing when we are weak, just how strong our God is.

Deciding not to harbor resentment was a pivotal moment in our grief. Forgiving those involved was crucial for our family to move forward, even though the legal process did not provide all the answers we sought. Trusting in God's plan gave me a peace that surpassed understanding, allowing me to focus on healing and honoring Jeffrey's memory.

Throughout this journey, my involvement with the discipleship ministry Bible Study Fellowship remained a constant and powerful strength for me. Leading children in studying God's Word, even though I had lost a child, anchored me in His truths and provided strength through community.

Looking back, I am reminded of Ephesians 4:31-32 and the call to let go of bitterness. God's grace enabled me to forgive and find peace amidst our tragedy. Through it all, I have learned that while we may never fully understand why certain things happen, God always remains faithful. His love sustains us, and His promises give us hope beyond our circumstances.

To any parent facing the unimaginable loss of a child, I encourage you to lean on God's grace, seek support from loved ones, and hold fast to your faith. Though the journey may be fraught with challenges, God is with you every step of the way, offering comfort, strength, and the hope of eternal reunion with our loved ones. My prayer for you is that you find peace in God and ***trust*** and ***rest*** in the absolute truth that He is still good and will never leave you. He is faithful and will carry you through until you can walk again.

Jeffrey

From

Mike and Connie~

2 Corinthians 1:4-5

*He comforts us in our troubles, so that we can
comfort those in any trouble with the comfort we
ourselves receive from God. For just as we share
abundantly in the sufferings of Christ, so also our
comfort abounds through Christ,*

God is the Father of compassion and the God of all comfort. In the
depths of our grief, especially after the devastating loss of a child,
He offers His compassion and comfort because that is who He is,
and He knows exactly what we need. But His gifts of comfort are
not meant to be kept to ourselves. He calls us to share the comfort
He has given us, so that the comforted become the comforters.

In this way, God never wastes our suffering. He uses our pain,
our heartache, and our healing to transform us into instruments
of His compassion. The comfort we receive from Him becomes
something we can offer to others who are walking through similar
darkness. Your story, your journey of healing, has the power
to bring hope and encouragement to those who are hurting in
the same way. God takes our brokenness and uses it to create
something beautiful, helping us share His love and grace with
others who are in need.

Chris

By Phil Martin,
His Father

It's amazing how God prepares you for even the most challenging days of your life. As I look back, I can see that He moved within our family even through the death of our beloved son, Chris. My wife, Brenda, and I grew up in faith-filled families. We had accepted/professed a personal relationship with Christ early in our lives, but as Chris grew into his teenage years, he was the one who took the spiritual lead in our family. I was wrapped up in the business world, fishing, and just doing guy things in the material world. Chris and I enjoyed all the fun things, from fixing trucks to yard work and just doing life. But Chris's faith was different. He was all-in with his faith, while I was dabbling. I had one foot in and one foot out. Even though Chris was my son, *he* was the one who impacted and led our family spiritually. I knew God wanted more and knew the truth, but I was apathetic and distracted by the world. I felt God was tugging at my heart to step up and lead my wife and son, but I resisted. Then we received the worst news of our lives: Chris, at 16 years old and a sophomore in high school, had been taken way too soon in an automobile accident.

That very tragic moment was the defining moment of surrender in my life. As we received the unbearable news, my wife and Amy, Chris's sister, fell to the ground in agony and shock. It's hard to explain, but I remember looking up to Heaven and, by the power of the Holy Spirit, making a choice to surrender. Somehow, I knew there was only one way my family would survive this agonizing pain. Like Chris, it was my time to surrender to being all-in with Christ. I know many people's response to tragedy is to blame God, but by His grace, I knew there was no other way through it all but to trust Him. I chose to believe He would be enough to carry us and somehow use this horrific pain for good.

As I remember Chris, I can't help but smile. Chris was an incredible young man for his age. He had a deep love for his friends and family and enjoyed doing things for them all. His heart was big, and I'll share a couple of stories that exemplify it. One morning, Chris and I left for the deer lease. We had been gone only a short time when my phone rang. Brenda called me to thank me for the cash I left her on the kitchen counter. I told her I didn't leave it, but I looked over at Chris, who could hear the conversation, and he smiled. He knew his mom never carried much cash and didn't want her to run short while we were gone for the weekend. He was always thinking about his family. His sister, Amy, shared with us that Chris had been sending her money while she was at college. While in school, he DJ'd parties with music, lights, and decorations, mowed yards, and worked at Calloway's Nursery so he could be generous with his money. What 16-year-old kid does that?

Another day, Chris called me at work asking how to start the Jeep belonging to a friend from out of town. She wasn't supposed to leave town, and now her Jeep wouldn't start. We tried several things until he fixed it. He didn't want her to get in trouble, so he stayed until it was fixed, even though it made him late for DJing a party he had booked that night.

I also remember returning home from a hunting trip to be greeted by Chris bounding out excitedly to the truck. His eyes were bright with pride as he showed me what he had been up to. He had rigged up a long extension cord over the roof to power his intricate outdoor Christmas lights, ensuring safety by installing a waterproof outlet. However, my heart skipped a beat when I saw he had tinkered with the breaker box, exposing the main power supply. Concerned, I warned him about the potential danger of touching the wrong wires. But Chris assured me that he had done his homework and that his grandfather had taught him a trick: as long as you didn't touch the white and black wires simultaneously, you'd be fine. That same year, he wired the outdoor kitchen we were building together. Here was my son, displaying skills and knowledge beyond his years, and he definitely knew more about wiring than I did!

Chris did things that seemed so mature for his age. He regularly used the Weed Eater at his grandparent's gravestones at the cemetery because he didn't think the groundskeeper did a good enough job. Many adults said they enjoyed conversing with Chris because he talked about things on an adult level and rarely about himself. He had a generous soul and thought about things most 16-year-olds would never think of. Looking back, Brenda and I thought Chris truly lived the sixteen years of his life to the fullest.

Losing a child absolutely changes everything. It definitely tests your faith. There really is no way out of it. When you cannot answer the question "Why," the only question is, "Who" will you turn to? Would I still believe that God was good? Could I trust Him, though our hearts were shattered into a million pieces? Thankfully, we both chose to submit our lives to the only one who controls our eternal souls. We had become too rooted in this life for the previous decade and drifted from our daily dependence on Him. When we lost Chris, I knew there was no other way to make it through and chose to be all in with the Lord. The Holy Spirit had prepared me to say "yes" in that crushing moment. It was a "yes" to choosing to trust God and follow Him in the darkest nights of our souls. Second Corinthians 1:4-5 became my hope.

He comforts us in all our troubles so that we can comfort others. When they are troubled, we will be able to give them the comfort God has given us. For the more we suffer Christ, the more God will shower us with His comfort through Christ.

The grace and mercy I found in God was truly enough. It became a purpose that I would have never chosen, sharing my story of loss and grief empathetically with others. And today, as I look back at the years of ministering to others who have walked through the depths of this pain through ministering in grief groups and church, I stand in awe of the Lord's comfort for broken hearts. He meets each person in their grief and will walk with you every step of the way.

Brenda and I found that, as a rule of thumb, people who have lost a child genuinely want to only hear from someone who can relate to them on a very deep, empathetic level. We have been able to share with broken hearts that although God didn't cause it, He will use it to draw us to Himself, the Comforter. He did it with Brenda, me, and Amy. Chris's death caused me to cling to the only One who could carry me through the dark. I didn't understand and asked all the "Why's?", but I went back to the truth of who God is: He is faithful, just, good, and sovereign. He is the One who will carry you through grief. God is big enough to take our questioning, and strong enough to help us through it.

Many cannot surrender immediately in the moment of loss. Still, they will ultimately realize that He alone is the resolution to surviving it all. I decided to believe and be determined in my faith, and that kept me from getting stuck in grief. That is my heart for anyone who has experienced the loss of a child. He truly is the anchor that will hold you together. As I lost my precious wife recently, I found God to be faithful still. My goal is to finish this earthly journey strong.

A lot of people think, "Why didn't God save their child?" I understand, but everything is sifted through God's hand. Nothing catches God off guard. In the book of Job, God allowed tragedies to happen, but He didn't cause it. This is where faith is born. How else would we know that God is strong, mighty, and sovereign enough to overcome any situation with good if we didn't experience the trials of life? God is over all and works in the most difficult situations. Yes, we don't know why bad things happen, but we can know WHO is over it all. He is good, just, and righteous, and He uses all things to accomplish His purposes. God never abandons one single aspect of Himself; He works all in unison to accomplish His purposes throughout eternity.

Of course, when you lose a child, you lose their future, leaving you wondering who they would have married, what their children would grow up to be, what they would have done for a living, and most importantly, how they would walk with the Lord. We are so thankful that Chris had accepted Christ two years before his death and lived so intentionally for Christ from that point on. Now he is by the Father's side, so there is a little bit of Heaven in our home! What a gift it was to be the parents of an exceptionally good young man who was taken way too early. We are grateful for the time we had with him and look forward to eternity with him. That is how we can say that God is good in all things!

I want to express that the Scriptures became crucial in knowing God's grace-filled love for us. We relied on His Word to comfort us, reminding us that death in this life is but a temporary pain, and that He offers us the opportunity to live eternally with Him and our loved ones.

I am grateful that God allowed us to be Chris's parents. I don't just hope, but I know for sure that we will be reunited with him in the amazing bliss of the Lord for eternity. I have held onto Philippians 4:13, which promises I can do all things through Christ who strengthens me! Second Corinthians 4:18 has kept my gaze on Christ as we walk our earthly journey, *"So we fix our eyes not on what is seen, but what is unseen. For what is seen is temporary, but what is unseen is eternal!"*

God has healed us through our loss and equipped us to reach out to others, comforting them by pointing them to Jesus. I am confident that God did not cause Chris's death, but He did allow it. I have since learned it is because of sin entering the world that we have pain and suffering. Still, we have an amazing God who not only brings us through our grief but provides us peace in this life, knowing the fear of death does not own us. Life's hardships provide an opportunity to seek God, see Him work in our lives, and trust His greater purpose. When I made sharing the gospel of Jesus Christ my purpose in life, my grief became less, and my peace grew until my focus was on serving Him and not the things of this life.

I now know death is simply passing through a doorway into His perfect presence forever! I encourage you to live one day at a time, becoming the person God created you to be. God is still in control, and His love for you knows no bounds and reaches into the depths of your pain. He created us to bring Him glory! He will never leave you alone, so you can trust Him totally with your pain.

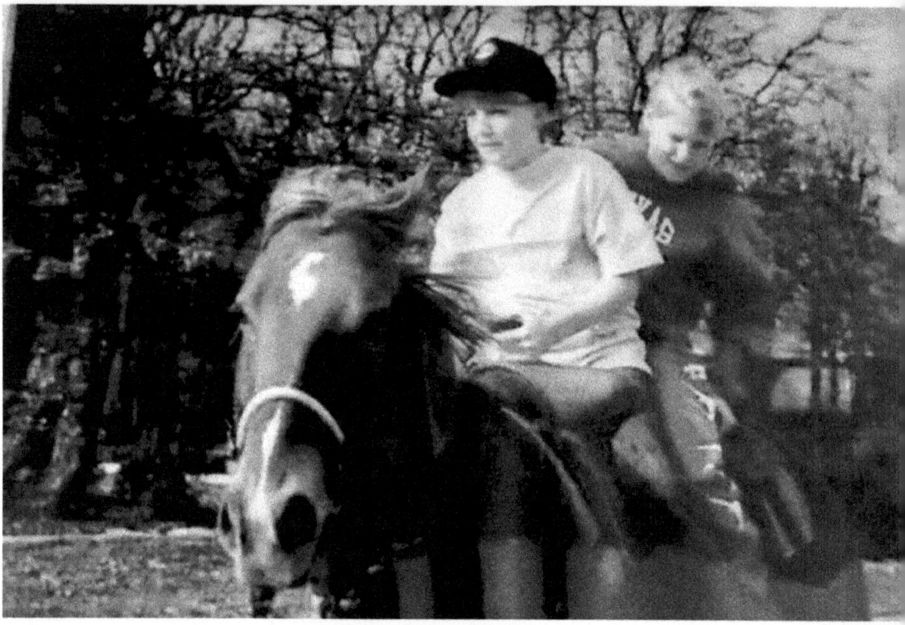

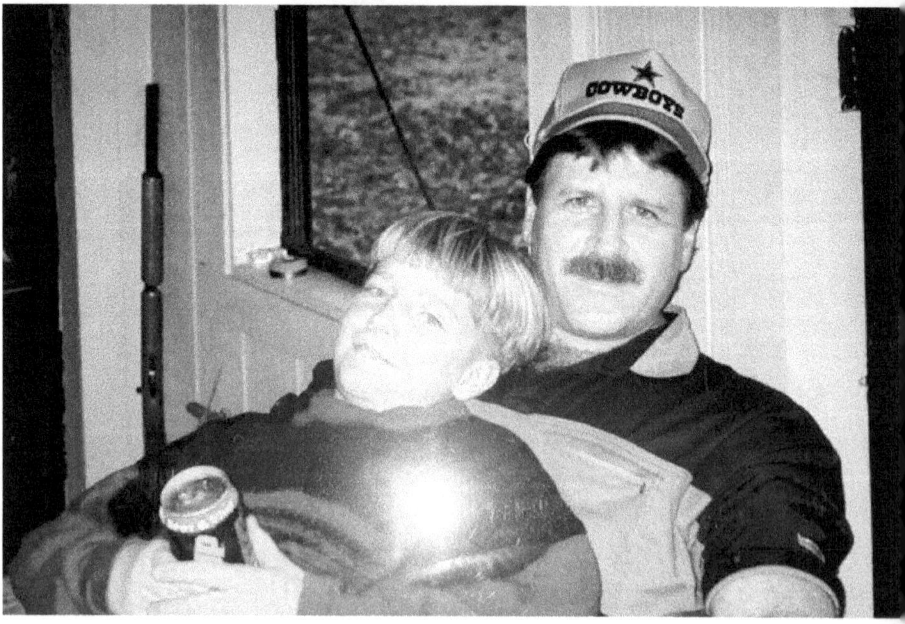
COWBOYS

From

Mike and Connie~

James 1:12

*Blessed is the one who perseveres under trial because,
having stood the test, that person will receive the
crown of life that the Lord has promised to those who
love Him.*

We have an enemy who seeks to overwhelm us with the weight of our trials, trying to break us under the heaviness of our grief. He challenges everything we know about God's love and goodness, aiming to shake our faith. But those who persevere, who hold fast to the truth with steadfast endurance, will not be defeated. They remain anchored in God's promises, and in the end, they will receive from Him the crown of life. Even in the darkest moments of your grief, as you press on with unwavering faith, God is with you, strengthening you, and His reward awaits you—a promise that He will never let you walk this path alone.

Naomi Vashti

By Zach & Tammy Woltersdorf,
Her Parents

Our Story

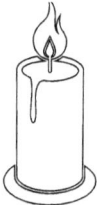

Life, we've come to realize, is much like a stained-glass window. This analogy has become one of our favorites because it so beautifully reflects how God shapes the story of our lives. Each piece of the window, each moment, adds more color and depth as the years pass. As we look at our family, we see how every member fits into the mosaic God has designed, and how each memory we've made together has become a part of this beautiful, unfolding story.

This is our stained-glass story, but it's not just ours—it's His story. It's God's work in our lives, a story of grief, redemption, and healing. We've watched, over time, as He tenderly mends the broken pieces of our window, especially the pieces shattered that day when we lost our precious Naomi to suicide. We see God at work, gently restoring the pieces with His love, His grace, and His healing blood. Every day, He is putting the window of our family back together—piece by piece.

Our stained-glass family is a reflection of God's love, and it has been shaped over the years. We were married in 1991, and in the following year, we welcomed our first child. Over the next 33 years of marriage, we were blessed with twelve children—five boys and seven girls. Naomi Vashti, our sweet Naomi, was number eight in the birth order. Her name means "peaceful, beloved," and she was seventeen when she left us. Naomi was the fifth girl, with four sisters and three brothers ahead of her, and two younger brothers and two little sisters after her.

Naomi was always such a sweet, shy little girl growing up. She had the most beautiful golden hair, with the cutest little curls, and she was always right by Mom's side—her shadow. But then, when she was almost two, her little brother Israel arrived, and their bond was something truly special. They were inseparable. As they grew, Naomi became quite the tomboy—something we never quite expected—but it led to so many wonderful adventures with Israel. They would have airsoft wars, ride bikes together, and share their love of music. Their connection was pure, and we'll always cherish the memory of their laughter and shared moments.

Naomi was always the strongest of the girls, and that strength really shone through as she grew older. By the time she was old enough, she'd join us on the hay crew every summer, working tirelessly alongside the rest of us. She had a natural talent for working with cars, and she was the only one of my children who was driven enough to earn her own money to pay for driving school. In fact, she was the first to get her license at 16 years old, a milestone she worked so hard to achieve. Naomi also had the most beautiful voice. Zach, her dad, heard her sing for the very first time the day she passed. Since then, we've been blessed to hear her voice a few more times, thanks to some recordings she made.

Naomi was generous and kind-hearted, always giving her time and energy to help around our property. She worked so hard that when she was gone, it felt like the work piled up and became overwhelming.

In April of 2022, we decided to take a family vacation to Lincoln City to celebrate Zach getting a new job. After years of working for himself as a General Contractor, this was a big change for us, and we wanted to mark it with something special. We rented a large Airbnb to fit our whole family—five kids still at home out of twelve, making sure there was enough room for our adult children and their families, too.

It was a Saturday, the last full day of our stay. The kids all went to town to have coffee and do some shopping. Naomi and her sister had a small disagreement earlier that morning about a hairbrush, and the tension between them lingered throughout the day. Despite that, Naomi found a pair of cool Vans at the outlet stores and treated herself to them.

When everyone came back, we packed up and headed to the beach to watch the sunset and have a bonfire, something Naomi had been really looking forward to. She had even loaded all the wood into the truck before we left for the weekend, making sure we had everything we needed for the night. But when we arrived, it was clear that something was bothering her. She and her sister still hadn't fully resolved their earlier disagreement, and Naomi seemed agitated. Lydia tried talking to her, but it only seemed to make things worse, so Naomi decided to take a walk down the beach alone. Their mom told Lydia she'd talk to her when she came back.

When Naomi returned from her walk, Tammy and Naomi sat off to the side, just the two of them, and talked for a little while. She doesn't remember all of the details of their conversation— it's a blur now—but they spoke for about twenty minutes. Zach came over to check in on the conversation, offering his own words of encouragement. He reminded Naomi to focus on the good things, and he urged her to help get the bonfire going. We both hugged her, and Zach told her he loved her with a big warm hug and a kiss on her forehead. As we parted the last thing she said to Tammy was, "We're not friends, remember, Mom." She had told all of our kids at one point that while we are always there for them, as parents, we also have to maintain the role of guiding them, even as they grow older and seek more independence. It was a conversation we'd had many times with all our children, but hearing it from Naomi that night broke her heart in a way she can't fully explain.

Zach gave her a long, tight hug and told her he loved her, too. Naomi reluctantly got the fire going and we all settled around the flames to watch the sunset. Naomi had always loved sunsets—they seemed to calm her spirit. We took a family photo, and then we headed back to the Airbnb, tired but content after a beautiful evening.

Little did we know, that would be the last time we would all be together like that. The next day, Naomi would be gone. I will forever treasure that last night, the love and the laughter, even in the midst of the tension. It was a night full of bittersweet memories, and though we didn't know it then, it was the last chance we had to tell her how much we loved her.

***

From Tammy

I was in the kitchen, preparing some snacks, while the house was filled with laughter and conversation. We were enjoying the hot tub on the back porch, and I remember Naomi hollering from the loft (where she and her siblings were taking pictures with each other) and asking "Mom, where are your bathrobes?" I thought she must have wanted to use one for the hot tub. Her sister, Lydia, heard the request and went to help Naomi find one of them. Then she (Lydia) and her boyfriend went for a walk down to the lakefront, just a two-minunite walk down the hill.

A little while later, I was playing a board game with Israel when her sister, Esther, came into the room, asking if anyone had seen Naomi. We suggested that maybe she had gone down to the lakefront with our other daughter, who had left minutes earlier. Esther decided to go look for her.

A few minutes later, Esther returned, visibly more anxious. She was adamant that we needed to find Naomi right away. She went to the bathroom door, but it was locked. She started pounding on the door, calling Naomi's name, and began to panic when she couldn't open it. Israel rushed over to assist her as well.

I rushed to the kitchen to grab the key, my heart racing as I tried to stay calm. I unlocked the door, and that's when I found Naomi. She had hung herself by using the bathrobe belt she'd asked about earlier. We did everything we could to save her. My son and I immediately started CPR, but as I tried to breathe life into her, I knew she was already gone. I remember going into a rage I had never thought possible. It felt like an out-of-body experience. Esther ran to wake my husband, who had been sleeping downstairs.

***

162

From Zach

That night, I was sleeping downstairs with our dog, Belle, when I was suddenly jolted awake by Esther, her voice frantic and full of panic. "Dad! Dad! Something terrible has happened to Naomi! You have to help her, we need your help, wake up!" She had run downstairs, screaming, trying desperately to wake me.

I rushed upstairs, not fully understanding what was happening, and that's when I saw Naomi on the bathroom floor. Her brother was performing CPR, his face full of terror and determination. My heart stopped in my chest—I couldn't believe my eyes. I took over from him, my hands trembling as I worked to keep her alive until the paramedics arrived. When they did, they had to pull me away, but I kept pleading with them, begging them to help her. I thought I heard them say she had a heartbeat, but as they loaded her into the ambulance and drove off, I felt my heart sinking, knowing deep down that something was terribly wrong.

At the hospital, I was met by the nursing staff at the door. They told me, gently, that Naomi hadn't survived. In that moment, I was in complete denial. I shouted at them, "You're not sorry! Get out of my way, I'm going to see my daughter!" I couldn't process it. I couldn't accept it. But when I walked into that room, the reality of it hit me all at once. I collapsed by her side, shaking her, trying to wake her up, begging her to come back to us, to just open her eyes and go home.

Tammy arrived a little while later, after the police had gone to get her and inform the rest of the family. When she walked into the room, neither of us could hold it together any longer. We just cried, holding each other, comforting one another. In that moment, it felt like everything was broken. Tammy finally convinced me to leave.

I still remember the crushing feeling in my chest—the guilt, the overwhelming sense of failure. I thought I had failed as a father, that I had somehow let Naomi down. I felt like I had given up on her. I was completely broken.

When we got back to the Airbnb, I went to the couch, hoping to sleep and escape, but the weight of everything from that day—the horror, the helplessness—kept me wide awake. I just wanted the nightmare to end. But then, as if on cue, Belle, our puppy, came to me. She gently placed her paws on my face, nose to nose, with tears running down her face. To this day, she still does the same thing. She stays close, watching over me until I fall asleep, then moves down to my feet, guarding me as I rest.

***

Zach's journey to healing

After Naomi's passing, the cracks of grief began to appear in all of us. For me, it was like the weight of it all was too much to bear.

I started drinking heavily every night, trying to numb the pain, the regret, and the anger that consumed me. The flashbacks of that night haunted me relentlessly. I had just started a new job, and it was hard for me to focus on anything with the constant swirl of thoughts about that day, about what happened to Naomi, and the hole it left in our hearts. I was angry—angry about her death, angry at how it had touched all of us, and angry that we couldn't change what had happened. The pain was overwhelming for all of us, and in many ways it felt like we were drowning in it, trying to hold on to each other and to life, but struggling to stay afloat.

Before Naomi's death, I was just going through the motions, following Christ out of routine. I grew up in church, becoming a Christian in 1996. At that time, the Lord moved powerfully in my life. I felt a deep, burning desire to be on fire for Him—

to be purified like gold in the refining fire of His presence, so I could be made clean and used by Him. My friends warned me that this wasn't something I should wish for, but it was exactly what I wanted. However, as trials, disappointments, and struggles piled up over the years, a deep silence began to settle in. I found myself drifting further and further away from the Lord, unable and unwilling to hear His voice.

For fourteen long years, I searched for God, longing to know His will, yet it felt like He had become silent. Looking back now, I realize it wasn't God who was silent—it was me, retreating in frustration, not knowing how to hear Him or connect with Him. Psalm 63 has been a life chapter for me since I first came to know the Lord. I would cry out in anger, holding onto God's promise to seek Him, but I couldn't hear His response. His promise gave me a sense of comfort and direction in a dry and weary land, but I felt like I was missing His voice. I felt as though I was out of His will, and that somehow, all the tragedy in my life—especially with Naomi's passing—was the result of that.

Watching my adult children make choices that seemed to pull them further from God only deepened my sense of loss and confusion. I felt cursed, like I couldn't escape the weight of the sorrow that seemed to hang over me. I would go to church, hoping for healing, but the grief and anger I carried toward God were so overwhelming that I often had to leave, unable to bear the weight of it all.

It took losing Naomi and two long years of grieving for God to finally break through. My wife, Tammy, signed us up for a retreat for grieving parents—the *While We're Waiting* retreat. It was held at the beach during the same week as the second anniversary of Naomi's passing. When she told me about it, I was hesitant and skeptical, but she felt deep in her heart that it was God's timing.

165

At the retreat, I felt God tugging at my heart in a way I hadn't felt in years, especially regarding my unresolved anger and hurt over Naomi's death. I knew I needed to deal with it, but it was hard. During that time, I felt God leading me to the beach. It was a step of faith I didn't want to take, as it triggered memories of that night—of Naomi leaving us at the beach. I couldn't bring myself to go for the longest time. It took me 45 minutes to even take a step, so overwhelmed by grief that I thought I'd break down. But finally, I walked down to the ocean, and as I stood there, I felt the Lord speak to my heart, saying, "See? That wasn't so bad."

That moment was pivotal. It was at the retreat that I also felt the Lord calling me to forgive Naomi. Not just for what she had done, but for how deeply it hurt all of us—how it shattered our family. It was the pain of our love for her and the way she left us that made it so hard to move forward. I struggled with that grief, not just because of Naomi's death, but also because, in those early months, many people grew silent. Some stayed away because they didn't know what to say, and others didn't know how to comfort us. We had just started attending a new church, and being so fresh into the congregation, we were now known as "the family who lost a daughter to suicide." That was incredibly isolating. Even my own family—my mom and brothers—became distant. It was the loneliest time of my life.

In the months that followed, I lost my job after two years and four months of employment. At the time, it felt like another blow, but looking back, I see it differently. It was as if God had removed that job so I could finally grieve His way. I had been using my job and alcohol as ways to numb the pain, to avoid facing the shame and guilt I felt for not being the father Naomi needed. Losing that job forced me to slow down, to stop running, and face my brokenness.

Then, in the next two months, the Lord really opened my eyes to the self-destructive behavior I had been caught in. For the first time in years, I could hear His voice again, guiding me, speaking truth to me. One day, I had a revelation. I felt like I was standing on the edge of a great precipice, looking down into a cavern that seemed too deep and dark to cross. It felt hopeless, like there was no way forward. It reminded me of a scene from *Indiana Jones and the Last Crusade*, where Indiana faces the leap of faith over a deep chasm, unsure if the path is there.

I felt the Lord asking me to take a step of faith, even though I couldn't see the way forward. The Lord was inviting me to trust Him, to take that step even though the path seemed invisible. What I saw in that moment was the cross—His cross, the one He had died on for me. And I realized that the step of faith I was being asked to take was to trust in the blood He shed for me. It was a powerful moment of surrender; I felt healing begin to work in my heart.

Through this journey, I've begun to feel the Lord's touch in my life again. I'm finding hope, hope that this pain and suffering are not in vain but are for His glory. That Sunday at the retreat was the first time in a long while I was able to sing praises, to worship with tears—not tears of sorrow, but tears of joy—and love for my faithful Savior who has never left my side. Through all the pain, He has been there, and I'm learning to trust Him again.

***

Tammy's journey to healing

The day after Naomi passed, when we returned home, I felt like I was in a fog—lost, unsure of what to do next. Honestly, though, I can say that without the support of some very close friends, I think we'd still be emotionally stuck in Lincoln City. It was their help that pulled us through.

It reminds me of something I've thought about often: in every church, the stained-glass windows tell stories—familiar Bible stories—but each one is unique. Each depiction of Christ's life is a tapestry, woven with both joy and sorrow. My story, especially in the years after Naomi's death, is different from Zach's, but it still tells that same story—of joy and sorrow, of healing and grief, as we tried to move forward from that day.

To our surprise, word of Naomi's passing spread quickly, and by the time we got home, there were people already at our house—mostly youth. Looking back, I'm actually grateful for that. As hard as it was, I felt the Lord guiding me through those early moments. He was asking me to do the hard things, to face the grief and pain head-on. So, I began talking to anyone the Lord highlighted to me, asking them to share their stories of Naomi, especially the last months, weeks, even days of her life. I wanted to understand, to grieve with others who had also known her, while being present for my kids who were so distraught.

That first year, all of our children came home. We faced every "first" without Naomi together as a family, each of us trying to find our way through the pain. I commited myself not to drink or use any substances that year. In hindsight, I think part of that decision was driven by guilt—guilt for having had a drink the night Naomi died. We had made some piña coladas, and I couldn't shake the "what if"—what if I hadn't had that drink, maybe I would have seen her go into the bathroom, maybe I could have done something to save her. But I knew I had to feel everything. I had to do the hard work of healing, grieving, and being present—not only for myself, but for my children, who were falling apart emotionally.

Our new church embraced us during this time, and we were able to get the counseling we needed. The Lord was faithful in providing financially so that we could receive help. That first year, all I could do was show up at church. I couldn't sing. I couldn't lift my hands. All I could do was weep. The songs, the messages about a good God, felt impossible for me to accept at that point. It shook me to my core. I was angry, confused, and my faith felt like it was crumbling beneath me. But slowly, I began to step out in faith. I started saying yes to the Lord's leading, getting involved in church activities, serving others, and making new friends. I didn't have all the answers, but I was trying to walk through this grief alongside my kids.

As the months passed, memories would come rushing back. Our phones would flash reminders of her birthday, her photos, our shared moments. We would laugh, then cry, as we marked the 23rd of each month—going to her grave, placing flowers, counting the months since she was no longer with us. But as the second year arrived, it seemed like everyone—especially our adult children—had to get back to their routines. The house grew quiet, and the weight of Naomi's absence hit me in a new way. I felt very alone. It seemed like the friends who had been there for us in the beginning drifted away. As a result, I struggled with loneliness.

I'll never forget the chaplains who came to our house the day after Naomi's passing. They asked my kids, "Where was Jesus? Can you see Him? Where do you picture Him?" Some of my children said they saw Him standing behind them, or holding Naomi, or holding their hand. But I couldn't see Him. I could feel Him, but I couldn't see Him. It left me feeling lost and disconnected.

But then, something happened on the two-year anniversary, just a few weeks before we went to the *While We're Waiting* retreat. God brought to my memory my own childhood—how I had always wanted my father to show up at my sporting events, but he was never there. I always looked for him, but he never showed up. And in that moment, God revealed to me that my inability to see Him—really see Him—was shaped by that experience. Yet, despite not always seeing Him, I knew deep down that He was with me. His Spirit was with me, guiding me, walking with me through the pain.

One of the most healing parts of our journey has been Griefshare. We started attending just three months after Naomi passed. We brought as many of our kids as would come, and it was incredibly healing for us. Now, we're in our fourth round of Griefshare, and it's comforting to comfort others who are grieving, just as we have been comforted. Sharing our story, offering hope, and supporting others on their journey has been part of the healing process.

Each of our children has their own version of that night, their own traumatic memories of what happened, how they tried to help each other through it. We all went through that horrific night together, each of us finding our own way to cope, to comfort, and to survive. But the pain is something we will carry with us forever.

Often, people try to comfort me by reminding me that my beloved Naomi is in heaven, surrounded by our loved ones who will joyfully welcome us when we arrive. While I eagerly anticipate that glorious reunion, the Lord has gently highlighted an even deeper truth for me: in that moment, my focus will not be on those who greet me, but solely on the radiant face of Jesus. In my grief, I sometimes struggled to see Him clearly, yet during a Sunday service while singing the powerful song "Give Me Jesus," the line, "The blazing sun shall pierce the night, and I will rise among the saints, my gaze transfixed on Jesus' face!" resonated deeply within me. This beautiful reminder urged me to keep my eyes fixed on Him and His divine purposes for my life during this season of mourning. In my heart, I have found peace and strength in knowing that even in grief, Jesus remains my unwavering focus, guiding me toward healing and hope.

***

In Conclusion

In the days that followed, we were consumed with questions: *Why?* How could this happen? What was she thinking? Who knew what was going on in her mind? Why would God allow something so heartbreaking to take place? We were overwhelmed with questions. Could it have been the head trauma she sustained a month before? Naomi loved longboarding out on our country roads, and one day she crashed and hit her head so hard we had to take her to the ER. She spent over a week in bed with a headache. I couldn't help but wonder if that had anything to do with it.

Could it have been the drugs? We later learned that Naomi, wanting to fit in, had been given drugs and participated without our knowledge. Was it the abuse she suffered, the loss of friendships, or the bullying?

Naomi often felt left out, abandoned by her peers. Some of the friends she pursued treated her poorly, and she just wanted to be accepted by them. She would do anything to be part of their group, even if it meant putting herself in situations that hurt her. You could see the depression in her when she wasn't invited or included—she'd withdraw when she wasn't part of the activities; she'd try to mask the hurt, though we could see it in her eyes.

It was like some of those friends would intentionally exclude her, laughing as if they were in on some secret, knowing she'd find out and be hurt by it. I think we've all experienced rejection like that, but with Naomi, it seemed so much more painful. She was desperately longing for real relationships. We could see the pain that came with her need for connection.

Naomi had a hard time telling the truth, especially if she thought she might get in trouble or be hurt. She had a sharp tongue, and when she felt cornered or threatened, her words could cut deep. There were also wounds from her childhood—experiences we didn't fully understand at the time—that may have left scars too. We asked ourselves, "Why didn't we see the signs more clearly?" We wondered if there was something we missed, some way we could have helped her more. Was it guilt she carried inside? Could that have been part of the weight she was carrying?

We spent so much time talking to others, asking what they knew and when they knew it. There were so many cracks in Naomi's window that we hadn't seen. But God did. As hard as it is to accept, we believe in His providence, though we may never fully understand why.

The pain of the questions may never go away, but we trust that Naomi is in a better place now, free from the struggles and burdens that weighed her down here.

When trauma strikes, it's like a rock being thrown and shattering the stained glass. The cracks are real, but, over time, God uses His grace to repair the broken pieces. The glue He has used to restore us looks different for each of us, but it's been a combination of family, friends, community, and resources like Griefshare and *While We're Waiting*, Church on the Rock, and the Youth Group, that have helped to rebuild us. Our stained-glass window, our family, is much different than it was before April 23, 2022. But in many ways, it's more beautiful than we could have ever imagined.

The impact of Naomi's passing has unfolded in ways that can only be described as miraculous, touching the hearts of our children and the broader community. Shortly after her homegoing, one of our children committed his life to Christ, embarking on a transformative journey of healing and restoration. God has ignited a profound fire and hunger for His presence in Naomi's best friend and brother, Israel, who is now faithfully serving with YWAM at the Kona base in Hawaii. With a strong sense of calling, he is preparing for a mission trip to South Korea, fully embracing God's purpose for his life.

Moreover, several other children who had been grappling with unresolved hurts and stagnant faith have experienced a powerful revival within their spirits. Our Youth Director shared that for a time, the youth were merely going through the motions, but since Naomi's passing, there has been a remarkable shift. The youth group has not only grown in numbers but has also flourished with renewed fervor and passion for the Lord. It's a wonder to witness the transformation and spiritual awakening taking place.

Many youth and parents alike have testified about the profound moment they learned of her passing, recalling their feelings and experiences, how God used that heart-wrenching day to draw them closer to Him. It also brought an awareness for parents to pay attention to their own kids. Many have since stepped into ministries like YWAM and embraced various serving opportunities. The movement of the Holy Spirit among the youth has spilled over into our Sunday worship, inspiring the entire congregation and leaving a mark of His anointing. I am confident that God will continue to work through these events for His good and glory. Even as I share this, I hold onto the hope that it may bring healing to others who are grappling with loss.

We serve an extraordinary God—a God full of love, mercy, grace, compassion, and hope. It is our hope that sharing our story will bring healing to others, just as we have been healed.

In closing, I'll leave you with a poem I jotted down during this journey:

My heart broke that day
I unlocked that door
I rushed in to save her
I ran to get the knife
I cut her down to save her life
I tried to breathe life into my lifeless daughter

Where is the invisible hand of a loving God?

He's not done with me yet He unlocks my heart
He saves me
I run to him

He is the surgeon
He holds the knife
He breathes everlasting life

My heart remains broken
He holds her, He holds me, He heals my heart.

***

From Zach

As I reflect on all that I've learned through this journey—through the loss of Naomi and the many challenges that have followed—there are a few key facets of God that stand out to me, especially as a father. These lessons are not just for me, but for anyone who's walked through deep pain and loss. They are truths about God that have become anchors for my soul.

- **His Sovereignty**. I've learned that God is in control, even when life feels utterly out of control. His sovereignty means that I can trust Him, even in the darkest of times. I don't have to have all the answers, because I know He does. He sees the bigger picture, and His plans are higher than mine. This trust has given me peace, even when the road ahead seems uncertain.

- **His Compassion**. God's compassion is something I've come to understand in a deeper way. It means He is fully present with us, especially in times of need. He doesn't just stand at a distance; He enters into our pain with us. He weeps with us, He walks with us, and He holds us when we can't stand on our own. I've learned to be fully present for my children and those around me, as God has been fully present for me. His compassion has shown me what it means to love others in their pain, to listen, to hold space for their grief, and to walk alongside them.

- **His Grace**. Above all, I've learned that God's grace is abundant and unending. We can never outgive Him, and we can never earn it. His grace is freely given, no strings attached. It's not something we deserve, yet He offers it freely. As a father, this has been a humbling reminder that no matter my mistakes or shortcomings, God's grace is always there, covering me and my family. I've come to

175

understand that the more I experience His grace, the more I can extend it to others, especially to those I love most.

Through all the pain, the grief, and the moments of doubt, God has shown me who He truly is—He is sovereign, compassionate, and full of grace. And these truths, though hard-won, have been the source of healing for me and my family. I know we will continue to walk this journey of grief and healing, but I also know that we don't walk it alone. God is with us, and His love will continue to carry us through.

***

From Tammy and Zach

As we close this chapter of sharing our story, we know that God is not through with us yet; our journey of redemption will continue until the day of our own passing. We pray that our story will encourage you to keep leaning on Him. May you, too, experience the peace of trusting in God's sovereignty, the comfort of His compassion, and the strength that comes from knowing you are covered by His grace.

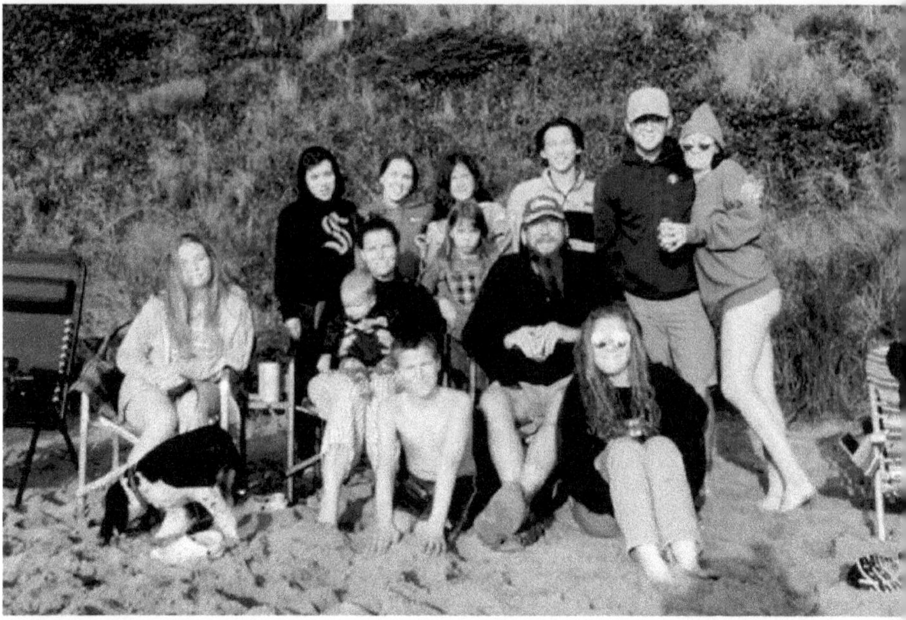

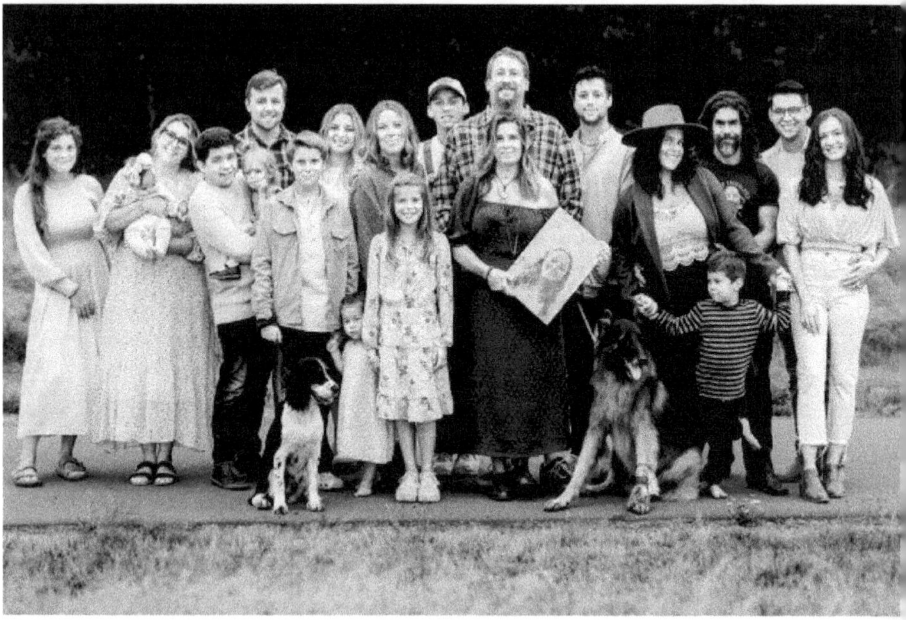

From

Mike and Connie~

Zechariah 13:9b

I will refine them like silver and test them like gold.
They will call on My name and I will answer them;
I will say, 'They are my people'; and they will say,
'The Lord is our God.'

God's refining fires are driven by His deep love for us. He desires to purify and refine us, not to harm us, but so that we can call on Him with a heart that is fully open to His presence—and so He can answer us with His unfailing grace. His ultimate longing is for us to be His people, in intimate, loving relationship with Him.

After enduring the intense suffering and hardship that grief brings, we can rest assured that God will always answer when we call on Him. He will be our God, and we will be His people—forever. He loves us so much that He will not spare us from the refining fires, because He knows that through the fire, we are shaped, strengthened, and brought closer to His heart. Though the pain is real and the road is difficult, know that His love is guiding you, and His presence will never leave you. Through it all, He is working to make you more like Him, and His faithfulness will carry you every step of the way.

Rebekah

By Regina Henthorne
Her Mother

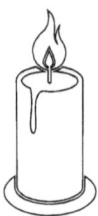

Some of the things I share might be difficult to hear, but I believe it's important for me to be completely transparent. My hope is that as you read this, you'll see the grace and hope that Jesus has brought into my life, even though I don't have answers to many of my questions.

Deuteronomy 29:29 (TPT) says, *"The Lord our God has secrets that are known to no one. We are not accountable for them, but we and our children are forever responsible for all He has revealed to us so that we may obey all the terms of these instructions."* There are secrets God has chosen not to reveal to us. Although He has not told us everything there is to know, He has told us all we need to know.

In 2009, my stepson was killed in a car accident. Then in 2011, my mother-in-law passed away, followed by my dad in 2012, and my father-in-law in 2014. In 2018, my marriage of 21 years came to an end. The series of losses seemed unrelenting. And then, on Wednesday, June 23, 2021, I received a text from my daughter saying she needed to talk. I stepped away from work to call her, and she said, "Momma, I guess I will move in with you." I had just relocated to Little Rock two weeks earlier.

"Okay, I get off at five and can be there by 7," I replied.

"No, Momma, let's wait until Saturday to make it easier for you."

"Babe, I don't mind coming when I get off."

"Mom, just wait, okay?"

"I love you."

"I love you too, Momma."

The next morning, around 11:30, I hadn't heard from Rebekah, so I sent her a text. Shortly after, I received a message on Messenger from someone at St. Vincent's Hospital asking for family. I didn't respond right away, thinking it might be another scam. Then, within 15 or 20 minutes, I got a call from the Monticello Police Department.

The officer on the other end said, "Is this Regina Henthorne?"

"Yes, ma'am."

"Are you in Monticello?"

"No, ma'am, I live in Little Rock."

"Okay, hold on a moment."

The silence that followed felt like an eternity. When she returned, she asked, "Can you be reached at this number anytime?"

"Yes, ma'am, I can."

"Okay, someone will call you."

"Wait, what's going on? Is my daughter okay?"

She said, "That's what someone needs to talk to you about."

The officer on the other end of the line ended the call, and my boss, seeing the panic in my eyes, immediately asked what was happening. He arranged for someone to drive me to the hospital. It only took 10 or 15 minutes, but in that moment, it felt like an eternity. As we were heading there, my sister called and asked for Rebekah's address. When I told her it was East Willis Street, she informed me there had been a shooting there—it was all over Facebook.

At around 7:20 that morning, Thursday, June 24, 2021, Rebekah was shot in the head by her fiancé's stepdad. That morning, the stepdad had gotten up with a gun in hand. He woke his wife and told her to gather the kids and go to the kitchen. As he moved through the house, he turned and shot his wife, narrowly missing her heart. He then turned and shot Rebekah in the head and also shot Harley in the stomach. In response, Harley managed to get his gun and shot and killed the stepdad. Harley's mom survived, but Harley did not.

Rebekah was airlifted to St. Vincent's. When I arrived at the hospital, the surgeon updated me on her condition, but I struggled to understand the gravity of what was being said. Desperate, I asked, "Is she going to live?" The surgeon solemnly looked at me and shook her head no.

From Thursday to Monday, I stayed by Rebekah's bedside, pleading with God to save her. I was there every moment, except when the staff insisted I step out. There were times when a tear would fall from her eye, and those moments felt unbearable. Planning a loved one's funeral while they are still warm is an impossible, heart-wrenching experience. I needed to see her eyes sometimes, so I would gently lift her eyelids and whisper, "I see you; Momma is here."

On Monday, June 28, I gave Rebekah her last bath, washing her as tenderly as I did when she was a newborn—her arms, fingers, legs, toes, face, and tummy. I was preparing my daughter for death the best way I knew how. On Monday, June 28, 2021, at 3:14 PM, she took her last breath.

***

Grief is an incredibly tough journey. My grandparents raised me, and their passing was one of the hardest things I've faced. I was in my early 20s at the time, and my faith wasn't as strong as it needed to be. When my stepson was killed, I felt like I might never recover. I was a bit older then and had a stronger foundation, but the loss was still devastating. Losing my dad was painful, but it didn't compare to the depth of anguish I felt with my stepson's death. And when Rebekah was murdered...it absolutely tested every ounce of strength I had.

I'm deeply thankful that my grandparents always had us in church. I grew up avoiding many of the pitfalls like drinking, smoking, or using foul language. But after Rebekah's death, I fell into a dark place. I attempted suicide and started using substances to numb the pain—vaping, drinking, smoking weed, taking pills, and even cutting. I'd wake up and start drinking right away, consuming at least a gallon and a half of mixed drinks and whiskey every day, along with marijuana and various pills. Being high and drunk meant I didn't have to think or feel. If I didn't think or feel, I didn't have to confront the pain of my reality or process what was happening in my world.

This destructive cycle continued for months. My days blurred together, but I never had a hangover or got sick from it. One day, someone remarked on how much I was drinking. I remember saying, "When I get sick from drinking, I'll stop." And then something shifted. When you leave the door open for God to work, He will. It felt like He was saying, "Challenge accepted!" The very next drink I took ended up with me sick on the floor.

While I didn't stop immediately, I can now say I am two years clean and sober.

I've heard people say that your life is shaped by the choices you make. While I see where they're coming from, I don't completely agree. For instance, I didn't choose for Rebekah to be murdered, a tragedy has undoubtedly changed my life completely. However, how I respond and the choices I make following her death are entirely up to me. I've used her murder as an excuse at times—there were days I was so overwhelmed with grief that I couldn't even get out of bed. Yet, I also recognize there were moments when I could have pushed myself harder and dug deeper. Instead, I let the tragedy of losing my only child give me a pass. I've given up so many times it's hard to count. I prayed and prayed for God to lift this burden from me, but it often felt like my prayers weren't being answered.

Eventually, I reached a point where I had to tell myself, "Regina, you're choosing to stay in this misery. Nothing you're doing is working. It's time to either stay where you are or try something different."

I used to tell Rebekah, "There's nothing you could ever do or say that would make me stop loving you." If we feel that way about our children, think about how much more Jesus feels that way about all of us! Joel 2:12-13 reminds us, *"Turn to me now, while there is time. Give me your hearts. Come with fasting, weeping, and mourning. Don't tear your clothing in your grief, but tear your hearts instead. Return to the Lord your God, for He is merciful and compassionate, slow to get angry, and filled with unfailing love. He is eager to relent and not punish."* His unchanging, relentless love pursued me.

One Friday night in February, during a revival, I hit my knees and prayed, "God, I'm so tired. I'm tired of running and living in misery. I'm laying this grief, anger, and misery at Your feet. You can handle it. Use it and me for Your glory. The way I'm going isn't bringing You glory, so here I am, use me." Within weeks, God reignited a calling He had placed on my life back in high school and added, "I also want you to lead a GriefShare ministry." Not long after, God made a way for me to follow this calling more easily by placing me in a new job in Star City, even though I was working in Little Rock at the time. It wasn't easy, but I learned that when God has a plan for you, He makes a way if you let Him work in your life. Ezekiel 36:26 says, *"And I will give you a new heart, and I will put a new spirit in you. I will take out your stony, stubborn heart and give you a tender, responsive heart."*

I want to share something with you that might resonate, especially if you're navigating the agonizingly painful journey of losing a child. When you say, "Here I am, use me," be prepared for some deep, often difficult self-reflection. I promise it will be worth it, but it's a tough path. You might find yourself needing to let go of things you hold dear—things that are wrapped in memories and love. For me and my good, God helped me let go so I could actually live again.

I remember a moment in church when I felt God nudging me to delete my daughter Rebekah's texts and contact info from my phone. It was such a heavy request, and it took me a week (and His grace) to muster the strength to do it. Later, I felt a stronger push to also get rid of her phone. I initially resisted, thinking I could just put it away on a shelf, but God's message was clear: I needed to let go completely.

It's such a painful process, letting go of tangible, physical reminders, especially when they hold so much emotional weight. I thought I could save a few pictures from Rebekah's phone, but as soon as I tried, it logged me out. I even thought about leaving the phone at the church altar and letting someone else deal with it. But God's message was, "You need to handle this yourself." He was mercifully stretching me.

There are moments when we're being asked to let go of things that we think we can't possibly part with. I had Rebekah's class ring, which I wore all the time. When God said it was time to let go of it, I felt my heart break. I thought, "This ring means so much to me." Was it hard? Did it hurt? Absolutely—it hurt deeply, but I have no regrets! Because He had asked it of me, He gave me the grace to do it, gently reminding me that letting go was part of my healing. (He'll never ask you to do something without providing the strength to do it!) It was something *that I needed to do* to let go because I held those things at a higher standard than I did Him and my relationship with Him.

It's incredibly hard and can feel so unjust. But sometimes, in letting go of particular things and obeying His voice, we make space for healing and growth. It's not about erasing memories or love; it's about finding a way to move forward with a heart open to new possibilities. I understand the profound sadness that accompanies it, while acknowledging what one person needs to do to find healing may not be the same for everyone; each journey is unique. For me, letting go of certain things was a necessary part of my path, but it doesn't mean that's what you must do. It's about finding what helps you move forward in your own way. Grieve deeply, hold onto your memories, and take your time with the process. What's important is following the gentle leading of the Holy Spirit.

A couple of months ago, I was driving home from work when I saw the most stunning rainbow—bright, bold, and beautiful. I wanted to snap a picture, but something told me to just take it all in. I watched the rainbow with tears streaming down my face, feeling deeply reminded of God's love, mercy, and grace.

A few days later, on my way to work, the sky was dark and cloudy. Out of the corner of my eye, I spotted a faint rainbow peeking through a small break in the clouds. It was there and gone in an instant. In that fleeting moment, I felt the Lord saying, "You'll have days when My presence is so obvious that there's no doubt I'm with you. But there will also be days when you have to search harder to feel My presence. It's not about punishment; it's about making you dig deeper and strengthen your relationship with Me. The more you seek, the more you'll understand and grow closer to Me." I am so thankful I can enjoy that kind of intimacy now, but it has been a journey.

I went through a period when I was so consumed by grief that I didn't care whether I ended up in heaven or hell—I just wanted to be with Rebekah. I even thought that if she was in hell, that's where I wanted to be. I was engulfed in darkness and the lies of the enemy; it was an incredibly painful place to be.

You might be wondering how I could have felt that way about my daughter, but honestly, I can't claim with certainty that she is in Heaven. There are many good people who don't make it to heaven; and it's a harsh reality that being good alone isn't enough. Accepting Jesus Christ as your Lord and Savior is the only way to make it to Heaven. My destination is Heaven, and it's not just about being reunited with our loved ones, but to be with my Savior—Jesus!

Thankfully, my focus is now firmly on Jesus. Knowing and having a personal relationship with Him is everything. While I deeply hope to see Rebekah again, He is my greatest hope and joy! If I am given the blessing of being reunited with her, that would be the most precious gift, but my heart is set on being *with Him* and trusting in His love and grace to guide me through this earthly life.

I know you've heard people say, "How you choose to live your life is entirely up to you." I used to find that statement incredibly frustrating. I would think, "You have no idea what I've been through." And while it's true that none of us choose the hardships we face, it is our choice how we respond to them. Perspective plays a huge role.

I could choose to live with a victim mentality—focusing on the pain of my parents' divorce, the feelings of inadequacy, the losses of my son, my dad, and my daughter. Or, I can shift my perspective and embrace a victor mentality. Instead of letting those painful events define me, I choose to focus on the blessings: the fact that my grandparents raised me in church and introduced me to Jesus; the twelve precious years I had with my stepson; the invaluable lessons from my dad; the nineteen years and 333 days I was able to share with my daughter. And above all, I am grateful that I am washed in the blood of Jesus and made fearfully and wonderfully. Psalm 139:14 says, *"I will give thanks and praise to you, for I am fearfully and wonderfully made; wonderful are your works, and my soul knows it very well."*

Jesus chose me, and He chose you, too. As John 15:16 reminds us, *"You didn't choose me, I chose you."* Bad things have been happening since the beginning of time. Sometimes they're the result of someone else's choices, sometimes our own, and sometimes they just happen. While the bad things aren't always our fault, how we respond to them is completely within our control.

Maintaining a perspective of gratitude and focusing on the positives, even amidst pain, helps in responding with resilience. Stay in prayer, immerse yourself in the Bible, listen to worship music, and engage with sermons throughout the week. When you stay spiritually nourished beyond just Sunday mornings, it's easier to keep a perspective of victory and stay focused on Jesus.

It's true that God will only do what you allow Him to do in your life. We all have free will to make our own choices, and sometimes that means forcing yourself to take steps you might not feel like taking. Let me encourage you that, if you find yourself struggling to attend church, then push yourself to go. If listening to worship music, reading the Bible, or tuning into sermons feels like a chore, then do it anyway.

You might wonder, "What's the point if I'm just forcing myself?" But here's the thing: when you force yourself to be in the presence of the Holy Spirit, you're opening a door for God to start working within you. It might not feel immediate, and it might not be easy, but as you continue, you'll find that what once felt like a chore can turn into something you genuinely want.

Over time, your heart can shift from a place of resistance to one of willingness. When that happens, you'll naturally make more room for the Holy Spirit to work in your life. Keep pushing forward, even when it's tough, and you'll start to uncover things about yourself and your faith.

It's important to remember that God's plan might not always involve quick fixes or immediate healing; that's okay. He still loves us, has a plan for us, and a purpose for our pain that can lead to blessings beyond what we could ever imagine. Often, God does choose to heal, but sometimes, He uses our difficult suffering to teach us and draw us closer to Him. In those dark moments, it's crucial to run *toward* God, not away from Him. Even in the midst of a storm, continue seeking Him and crying out to Him. You may be surprised to find that His presence offers comfort and understanding in unexpected ways.

I attended the 13-week Grief Share classes, and during one of our sessions, the topic of love came up. I shared that I had built walls around my heart because I didn't want to allow myself to love anymore—everyone I loved had left. I thought that if I didn't love, I wouldn't have to face heartbreak again. One of the ladies looked at me and said, "Ms. Regina, you aren't afraid to love because you are full of love; you are afraid to *be* loved." Then the facilitator asked me, "What do you do with the greatest commandments?"

Matthew 22:37-38 says, "*You must love the Lord your God with all your heart, all your soul, and all your mind. This is the first and greatest commandment. A second is equally important: Love your neighbor as yourself.*" If we live with a victim mentality, are we truly loving ourselves? The Scripture calls us to love our neighbor as ourselves, which means we need to love ourselves in order to love others properly. We are made in God's image, and He created each one of us. We have to care about and love ourselves. I never fully understood that loving myself was essential to loving others.

Forgiveness is another crucial part of this journey. When the Lord told me it was time to forgive the man who murdered my daughter, I can't fully describe the turmoil of thoughts and emotions that surged through me. Jesus still loved Judas, knowing what was to come. He loved the very people who were beating Him, and from the cross, He said, "Father, forgive them, for they know not what they do." If I can't forgive, how can I expect to be forgiven? Matthew 6:14-15 tells us, "*If you forgive those who sin against you, your heavenly Father will forgive you. But if you refuse to forgive others, your Father will not forgive your sins.*" We might never get the apology we think we deserve, but we are still called to forgive.

We also need to remember that accidents happen. While Rebekah's death was premeditated and not an accident, my stepson was killed in a car wreck. For a long time, I blamed the woman who caused the wreck. I know she didn't wake up that morning intending to cause harm. I hope that the man who killed Rebekah had one last chance to accept Jesus before his final breath.

Forgiving him was challenging, but forgiving myself proved even harder. As Momma, I felt I should have protected Rebekah. I constantly replayed the "could've, should've, would've" scenarios, and the guilt was suffocating. It made me physically, mentally, emotionally, and spiritually sick.

I remember reading the police report months later, describing how Rebekah was found, her hair over her face, breathing heavily. My first thought was that she might have been lying there wondering where I was—why wasn't I there to save her? The enemy feeds us endless lies; lies that can consume us. My hope now is that, in those moments, she cried out to Jesus.

When we were potty-training, I remember sitting on the edge of the bathtub, waiting for her to finish up. She was playing, as kids do, but then she suddenly got very focused on a spot just over my left shoulder. I knew she wasn't looking at me, so I glanced over my shoulder to see what had caught her attention, but there was nothing there. When I looked back at her, she was still fixated on that same spot. I asked, "Babe, what are you looking at?" She simply replied, "Him." Naturally, I turned around again, but still saw nothing. Curious, I asked, "Him who?" She said, "Jesus. He's right there. Can't you see Him?" That moment gave me chills. I'll always believe that she saw Jesus that day. The enemy knows our weak spots and will use anything to get to us. For me, my biggest weakness was Rebekah. I loved that girl so deeply, and I still love her, but the way I love her has changed. You see, Rebekah came before everything and everyone, even God. That wasn't how He intended it to be. Did my marriage end because of this? Possibly. Did Rebekah have to die because of it? That's one of those questions I don't have an answer to; maybe I don't really want one. But one thing I know for sure is that Jesus is full of love, mercy, and grace—enough for everyone. He wants us all to make it to heaven.

While we wait to see Jesus face-to-face, our job is to spread His word. I've been in church all my life, but I didn't have a real relationship with Jesus; I had religion. I was saved in high school, but I didn't build that relationship. I was too focused on following rules instead of truly connecting intimately with Him. Just like any relationship, it takes work. We need to communicate through prayer, reading His word, and worship.

Getting saved and building a relationship with Jesus doesn't mean life will be easy. Even with growth and healing, there are still tough days. It doesn't mean I'm weak or that I'm not progressing; it just means I'm having a hard moment. On those days, I often find myself on my knees, crying out to God. I might say something like, "God, it hurts. Everything feels so heavy right now. I don't understand. Please carry me. Let me feel Your arms around me. Thank You, Jesus, for Your love, mercy, and grace. Thank You for giving me back my life and a desire to live. Thank You for being worthy of my praise."

I've cried every night for the past 1,133 days. Nights and weekends are especially hard for me, but there's a joy in my heart that I can't quite explain. Lamentations 3:31-32 reminds us, *"For no one is abandoned by the Lord forever. Though he brings grief, he also shows compassion because of the greatness of his unfailing love."* If we stay close to Jesus, life can be bearable and even enjoyable. It takes effort on our part—He won't force His way into our lives. We have to want Him. We must be persistent in prayer and act on it. We are healed to help others, blessed to be a blessing, and saved to serve. This tragedy can become a triumph, but only if we allow God to embrace us. It won't happen if we just wait around. Sometimes, taking a small step can lead to a giant leap.

Even if I never see another prayer answered, Jesus is still more than worthy of my praise and worship. The fact that He saved my soul is *more than enough* reason for me to praise Him for the rest of my life. But here's the amazing part—He's done so much more for me, and He can do the same for each of you too! He longs to meet you right where you are and work in your life. Keep the faith, stay open to His guidance, and watch how He moves in ways you never imagined.

***

Rebekah's dad and I were sitting at the kitchen table early one morning, just a few days before Christmas. We were deep in conversation, discussing the gifts we had for her and trying to pick the perfect ones. Out of nowhere, her little head peeked over the back of the couch, and she giggled, saying, "Hey!" Her dad and I exchanged surprised glances before looking over at her. He asked, "How long have you been there?" With a playful grin, she replied, "Long enough."

On July 30, 2001, at 6:42 PM, we welcomed a beautiful baby girl into this world. On June 28, 2021, at 3:14 PM, that same precious girl took her last breath. God, in His infinite wisdom and purpose, knew she had been here "long enough."

For those of us who have felt the profound loss of a child, may it be a deep comfort to remember that God sees the full picture of our lives. Even when we struggle to understand, we can trust that His plans are *always* guided by love and purpose.

Genesis 50:20 reminds us, *"You intended to harm me, BUT GOD intended it all for good."*

Rebekah

Mike and Connie~

Psalm 73:28

But as for me, it is good to be near God. I have made the sovereign Lord my refuge. I will tell of all your deeds.

When you come to recognize the sovereignty of God over all things, it becomes the steady foundation that enables you to face even the most devastating storms life brings.

In the wake of losing my child, I chose to place my trust in God's sovereignty as my source of strength and comfort. In doing so, He became my refuge—the place where I found peace amidst the chaos, and where my heart, broken as it was, could rest. Even in the darkest moments of grief, He gave me the strength to speak of His goodness and to cling to the hope that He is in control.

God's sovereignty means that I could rest, knowing that He holds everything—every tear, every moment—in His hands. No matter how heavy the burden or how overwhelming the pain, I found that I could trust Him. And I want you to know that you, too, can trust Him. You are not alone in this. God is with you, holding you, sustaining you. God's sovereignty remains unshaken, and in it, you can place your trust completely, knowing that no matter how deep your grief, He is faithful and will never forsake you.

Paul Michael

By Connie Washburn,
His Mother

✝

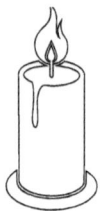

When Paul Michael was five years old, his daddy decided we would take him to his first football game. Since we lived so close to the Texas Christian University campus, he thought introducing Paul Michael to the sport of football would be a good idea. What he didn't realize was how impressionable a five-year-old boy could be. TCU knew how to catch their fans young and declared they would give out bobbing horned frogs to the first 100 fans. Just as promised, when Paul Michael reached the TCU gate, he was handed a nice-sized purple bobbing horned frog. He fell hook, line, and sinker for TCU! He carried that bobbing horned frog around like a trophy he had earned himself. That was all it took; his loyalty was now to the TCU Horned Frogs and had been ever since. His daddy (an Oklahoma University alumni) now had a job to do: damage control!

It was a beautiful September day, and our car was loaded. Today was it! The day of redemption! We were headed to Memorial Stadium in Norman, Oklahoma, to watch the OU/ TCU football game. We thought this game would be the one that would finally convert our son from being a loyal TCU Horned Frog to becoming an avid Sooner fan. OU was the pick and expected to squash TCU. "Today," my husband boasted, "you can become loyal to the right team, Paul Michael. You are about to now see who the true winners are!" Paul Michael's dad could hardly control his excitement. "Now, son," he said, "Every time OU makes a touchdown, the ponies will circle the football field." He gloated as he said, "You can expect those ponies will be getting lots of exercise today!" Paul Michael just grinned and smirked as he said, "We will see, Daddy; we will just see!"

We drove for four hours and finally arrived at Memorial Stadium. The parking lot was full. We walked towards the stadium and heard loud chants and laughter from cheerful fans. The smell of popcorn, hot dogs, and cotton candy filled the stadium. Over 84,000 fans divided the arena. One side wore purple tee-shirts and jerseys, and the other wore crimson red. Attendance was the largest on record for a Sooner home opener, and the third-largest crowd ever for a TCU football game. As we walked through the stadium, Paul Michael spotted the vendors selling the TCU official jerseys. "Dad, can I please get this jersey?" Paul Michael asked with enthusiasm. "I tell you what, son," his daddy smiled as he said, "if they win today, you can have that TCU jersey, but if they don't win, you can have one of those beautiful crimson red ones over there!" Paul Michael chuckled, feeling joy as he watched his dad's excitement over the game.

The football game was thrilling to watch! But it didn't turn out quite like the critics expected. TCU was playing smart and hard, and OU had fallen behind. When the game was over, TCU won! Paul Michael couldn't help himself; he looked at his daddy and said, "Well, those ponies sure didn't get much exercise today, did they, Daddy?" His dad couldn't help but join in on the laughter. Paul Michael loved his new oversized TCU jersey. It was the same jersey he would later be buried in.

He Was Ready

Paul Michael was the coolest, funniest, and most joyful child I had ever known. He had beautiful blonde hair and always wanted to wear it long like a surfer. However, after a certain point, I couldn't take it any longer and insisted on giving him a clean cut. Paul Michael enjoyed fishing, playing with Legos, and participating in sports. He absolutely "loved him some Jesus"! I often wondered how I was fortunate enough to be the mother of such a remarkable boy. I lived and breathed for that kid; he was my everything! His classmates adored him as well. His love for the Lord radiated through the way he lived.

When Paul Michael was in third grade, his private school introduced a new award called the Fruit of the Spirit. It was voted on by his classmates and peers, who chose the student they believed best represented the fruit of the Spirit in their daily lives. By the time Paul Michael reached fifth grade, he had already won the award twice. He truly was pure joy! His father once remarked that we never had a bummer day with him; he was absolutely right.

When Paul Michael was 11-years-old, he expressed his desire to be baptized. I wondered if he was too young to make such an important decision, so I consulted one of our elders, John. He took the time to meet with Paul Michael alone and asked him various questions about the commitment he was about to make. After their discussion, John returned and assured us that Paul Michael was definitely ready. It was clear that Paul Michael was wise beyond his years, fully dedicated to his faith, and eager to follow Jesus. Little did we know that five months later, Paul Michael would be standing in the very presence of the One he had just committed his life to.

Tragic Grief

It was the day before Mother's Day. I had to get up at 4 a.m. for an early morning shift. I dreaded going to work because I would miss another basketball game. Paul Michael's Saturday schedule was full. It started with an early morning basketball game, then off to paintball with his buddies, and ended with me taking him to the park fishing after my shift.

My twin sister lived next door. We both worked for American Airlines and had the same early morning shift, and planned to carpool to the airport. I was finishing my makeup's last touches when I heard a loud Bang! "What in the world!" I thought. I ran into the hall to see what had happened. Paul Michael had collapsed and was lying on the floor by his bedroom door. My husband was leaning over him, trying to get him to stand up. I asked, "What happened?" I could see Paul Michael's tennis shoes lying by the door and assumed he had tripped over them. My husband said," I don't know what's wrong. I heard him groaning and came to check on him. He said he can't breathe and doesn't feel well."

Paul Michael was sweating heavily. While we helped him to his feet, I asked my husband to turn the temperature down. As he went to adjust the thermostat, I gently helped walk Paul Michael down the hall. He said, "I need to go to the restroom," he was still sweating profusely. He sat down on the toilet and started dry heaves as though about to throw up. I said, "Sweetie, if you need to throw up, make sure you throw up in the toilet, okay?" I had no way of knowing his lungs were filling with fluid at that very moment. My 11-year-old boy was dying right in front of me.

I walked over to him as he sat on the toilet and combed my fingers through his sweaty hair. You okay, buddy?" I asked. Paul Michael never complained, not even when he was dying. He looked up at me, didn't say a word, just grinned at me with his dry lips. A few minutes later, he stood up and slowly walked out of the bathroom and into the hall. He said, "I feel better now." Still a little concerned about him, I said, "Why don't you come to our room and lie down with Daddy since I have to go to work"? Paul Michael slowly started walking into our bedroom and laid down on my side of the bed. I tilted my fan on the end table toward him to blow cool air on his little body. Paul Michael's last words were, "That feels good."

Realizing I was running late for work, I went to the bathroom to get my suit jacket. I walked back into the bedroom to tell Paul Michael goodbye and said, "Paul Michael, I'm leaving now; how are you feeling?" I touched his arm, and it fell over completely limp. "Is this some kind of a joke?" I thought to myself. Then I screamed, "PAUL MICHAEL!" My husband raised, asking him, "Paul Michael, Are you okay, buddy?" I ran to turn the light on. Paul Michael was white as a ghost with his eyes half shut. My husband yelled, "He looks dead!" We both started to panic. "Call 911!" I screamed in horror. I immediately started CPR, having no clue how to do it.

My husband tried calling 911, but the phone was dead. Panicked, he began screaming, "The phone doesn't work! The phone doesn't work!" The battery was dead, and we were both in complete panic. I grabbed the phone out of his hand and screamed, "Start CPR!" Then I started running down the stairs to go next door to my sister's house for help. Paul yelled, "I don't know how to do CPR!" I screamed back at him, "Then try!" I ran downstairs and swung the front door open, and my sister was walking over to carpool with me to work. I screamed as loud as I could, "CALL 911! Oh God, I think my baby is dead!" I quickly ran back upstairs to continue CPR. I was praying God would help me do CPR because I had no idea how to do it correctly. I continued pumping his chest, trying desperately to breathe my life into his. My brother-in-law Doug suddenly appeared with 911 on the phone. "Get him off the bed and onto the floor!" Doug was repeating the 911 operator's commands. I picked Paul Michael up and swung him around, laying his lifeless body on the floor. I continued CPR while Doug gave instructions. I looked up and saw tears in Doug's eyes. I was screaming inside, "What's happening?" My heart was pounding as I continued pumping his chest, shouting the counts as Doug gave them to me...1, 2, 3, 4, 5... breathe, breathe...1, 2!

I continued CPR until I heard my husband yell to the paramedics, "They are up here!" The paramedics were at my side, and I quickly moved out of their way. I stood up, feeling like I was about to faint. I started pacing in circles, praying, begging God for help! I pled with Him not to let my son die. My mind couldn't process what was happening; I was in a sea of confusion. In denial, I felt he wasn't going to die; he would be fine. I found myself screaming, "Oh God, I know you won't let him die!"

I ran downstairs where a fireman was on his knees praying with my sister. He said, "Can I pray with you?" I said yes, but as he started praying, all I could think of was getting back upstairs where my son was. I rushed back upstairs, and my husband said, "His lips aren't blue anymore!" "Blue lips? Oh, dear God, why are his lips blue!" The paramedics worked on him for what seemed like an eternity before strapping him onto the stretcher and carrying him downstairs. They wouldn't let me ride in the ambulance with them. The paramedic shouted, "Meet us at NRH hospital!"

I yelled, "No! Take him to Cooks Children's Hospital!" The paramedic yelled, "There is no time!" and shut the ambulance door. What did he mean by no time? It was all happening so fast, and my mind couldn't comprehend it. Only a short time ago, he was a happy, healthy boy. How could this really be happening? It made no sense. My mind refused to believe it.

We drove by my neighbor Melissa's house on the way to the hospital. Her 11-year-old son was like a brother to Paul Michael. Every day, Ethan was either at my house or Paul Michael was at his. They were two peas in a pod. I called Melissa, but Ethan answered; it was apparent I had awakened him. "Ethan, I said, it's an emergency; let me talk to your mother. "Hello," it was Melissa on the other end, "Melissa, it's Connie. I'm on my way to NRH Hospital. I'm unsure what's happening, but I think Paul Michael may die. Please call every person you know right now and get them on their hands and knees to pray. "Please hurry!" I cried. I thought if enough prayers were cried out, God would surely hear them. He would surely save him!

We arrived at the hospital at the same time as the paramedics. They rushed him back while the hospital staff led us to the chapel. My husband asked the staff taking us back, almost in an accusing tone, "Why are you putting us in the chapel?" He couldn't process what was really happening either. My head was racing, "Yeah, why are they putting us in the chapel? Do they think he is going to die? Oh God, please, I'm begging you, please don't let him die!" I prayed with everything I had. I didn't understand what went wrong. What's happening to my son? How can a healthy 11-year-old boy run races on field day and lie almost dead the next morning? The doctor came in and introduced himself. I asked him if he and his staff would please pray over my son. He promised me they would.

Melissa, Dave, and Ethan soon arrived at the chapel door. "Melissa, you brought Ethan?" I asked in surprise. I was concerned that Ethan was too young to be witnessing this nightmare. I knew Melissa had just seen Paul Michael the day before at field day and felt she must not believe it was as serious as it sounded. I mean, how could it be? Hearing the concern in my voice, she said, "It's okay, Connie." My sister Vickie asked them to join us in the chapel. We all joined hands, praying and pleading for God to save my son. The nurse walked in and said, "I'm just giving you an update to let you know your son is still the same." My husband said in a stern voice, "You mean to tell me my son isn't breathing?" The nurse told us Paul Michael hadn't breathed a breath on his own since he had been at the hospital. "What! Oh, GOD no!" I couldn't breathe and opened the door, running as fast as I could down the hallway. I had to get outside; I needed air! I fell to the ground outside underneath the tree at the emergency entrance. I looked up at the dark sky, sobbing, trying to breathe. I began screaming out to God again, "Please, Lord, I'll die without him," "Please have mercy, please save my son!"

As I was crying, it dawned on me that while I was outside, my son, the doctors, and my family were all inside. Panicked again, I ran back inside as it all became like slow motion. My family stood out in the hall, probably trying to figure out where I was. Melissa, Dave, and Ethan were behind the door in the chapel. I walked forward as the doctor approached us from the opposite side of the hallway. The doctor's face was tender; all eyes were on him. He looked at me and said, "I want you to know my staff and I prayed over your son as you asked us to, but I'm sorry, he's gone."

"NOOOOOOOOO! Oh, God, NOOOOOOOOOOO!" I screamed and felt myself sliding down the wall. It's hard to describe what happened at that exact moment. A supernatural feeling came over me. It was as though God had sent 1,000 angels to grab hold of me, and I was lifted back up the wall. I knew it wasn't my strength holding me up but the strength of the Almighty God. I suddenly felt a sense of calmness.

I asked to see him. They led us back to where my son was. He was lying on a silver medal table with the breathing machine still in his mouth. I walked over to him and held his hand. It was cold. My mind was still battling inside me. At one time, I thought I had seen him move. My sister was sobbing, and my husband was crying in disbelief. I felt like I wasn't there. I was suddenly in another world. I leaned over and kissed him. "Wake up now, my sweets, wake up...please," the tears running down my face tasted like salt. He looked beautiful to me. His blonde hair was so pretty. His ears were starting to turn a blue color; no oxygen, a sign of death.

"Oh baby, Mommy can't help you now, can I?" The tears wouldn't stop and were obstructing my view. After a few minutes, my sister said, "Connie, the lobby is full of people. What do you want me to do?" I said, "Bring them in to say goodbye." The lobby was packed. Where did they all come from? How did they all know already? It was barely 6 a.m. His teachers were there; his principal was there, and church people and a small group of people I had not seen in years were there.

Dr. Schecter, principal of their school, asked, "Would you like me to pray a blessing over Paul Michael?" When the prayer was over, Kelle, Kelly, Lisa, and I embraced each other. I remembered the day when our five boys chose the name "The Five Amigos." They were known to their peers for the next several years as The Five Amigos. Caleb, Tyler, Brady, Brett and Paul Michael. I said, "Now, there are only four amigos." We cried as we all stood there in disbelief.

I wondered how they would tell the boys their best friend was gone. My heart broke for the kids; I loved them so much. The room was empty again except for the family. The nurse said, "I'm really sorry; I want to give you all the time I can, but we have to investigate, and they need to take photos. You only have a few minutes left." I kissed him again, desperately wanting more time. How can I leave him, I thought? My mind was racing as I knew what they were about to do to my son's beautiful little body. I felt so helpless and knew his father did, too. I still couldn't completely process it. It was as though my mind was in denial and refusing to accept it. I knew it was true, but my mind couldn't comprehend its reality. I was in shock.

I walked outside the emergency room, to where the amigos' parents were discussing how they would tell the children. No one knew what to say to them because no one knew what had happened, including me. I told them details about the morning but had no answers on why or what happened that would take the life of an 11-year-old boy. As we were talking, I saw the paramedics pushing a stretcher with sheets covering a little body, transporting it into the ambulance. I knew it was him; it was my precious little Paul Michael. They were taking him to the morgue to do an autopsy. It was a scene I will never forget.

On the drive back home, I was quiet. I felt a strange sense of peace but thought I was having some out-of-body experience. I felt a calmness, which I knew was the Holy Spirit comforting me and giving me strength, but it was mixed with a painful sorrow deep enough to reach the ocean floor.

We later discovered the reason for his death. When Paul Michael was four, we took him to the doctor for a cough, and the doctor found a heart murmur. After more tests were run, they discovered he had a fistula (blood vessel) attached to his heart. The doctor said things like this were usually detected on a football field after death. We were relieved they discovered it early and could remove it. The doctors left a tiny area of the fistula in place, the part immediately attached to the heart. They assured us he was good as new and what could have been a deadly situation had been thwarted. None of us could have a clue that seven years later, a blood clot would form in that area and take my sweet boy's life anyway.

Spiritual Warfare

Looking back on all that transpired that awful day, I can't stress enough the importance of church, community, and support. Our pastor, church elders, and the community held us up when we couldn't stand on our own two feet, offering us prayers, forming food chains, and sometimes just sitting and listening to our grieving hearts. People kept coming in and out of our house all day, bringing food and drinks. While conversing with a church elder, I noticed Stephanie, one of the school kids' mothers, entering the room. She was carrying cases of paper goods. Kleenexes, paper towels, plates, napkins, silverware, coffee cups with lids, and loads of bottled water. She simply walked in, hugged my neck, carried in several loads, and walked out. She never said a word. It was as if she was saying it by her actions: I don't know what to say, but I love you! I remembered the day we took her son and several other kids to a sleepover at TCU. We all slept under the stars on the football field, watching movies and eating hot dogs. It was such a wonderful time. It would be the last time.

After everyone left, my husband and I were alone again. My thoughts kept going to the morgue. My son's body was in a freezer, and there was nothing I could do about it. The sky was dark, with lightning and thunder booming outside. The storms seemed to reflect what I was feeling on the inside. Darkness, fear, and feelings of hopelessness literally took me to my knees in agony. I couldn't speak; deep groans in between my sobbing were all I could get out. The pain was intense, and there would be no escaping it and no running from it. A spiritual warfare had begun raging inside me. It started with feelings of rejection and self-pity. I began to ask why. "Why him, God? He was working to be a leader for you. Why didn't you hear me when I cried out to you? Where were you, God?" I never questioned God's sovereignty but began questioning His wisdom and love for me.

Churches don't always know what to do in situations where a parent loses a child. After all, there isn't a one-shoe-fits-all guide to navigating this kind of grief. But the people who make up the church make a difference. In my case, it was one of the elders' wives. I wasn't close to Donna, but I greatly respected her. Not everyone can be a voice during dark days like these, but she decided to do "hard" with me. She jumped right in with both hands and feet to that dark hole that was desperately trying to devour me.

I have thought and searched for words that adequately describe the pain that accompanies grief, but there are none. I have discovered it is something you have to experience yourself to really understand. Words, tears, or descriptions cannot touch the depth of pain after losing a child. Therefore, we surrender it and carry it almost as a deep secret that can never be fully told. Grief can test one's faith to the very brink of one's soul. It will determine how solid the foundation is, and each person must decide if they will cling to their faith or allow suffering to cause them to rethink everything they have ever believed. It's where the rubber hits the road.

When Paul Michael passed away, I was a relatively new Christian. I had been studying scripture in Bible Study Fellowship class for about eight years. The decision to follow Jesus seriously became instrumental for me. I was thankful the foundation of my faith became solid before the bottom completely dropped out. Early in my grief, Donna began to mentor me in ways that only God knew I needed. This dear woman spent the next several years walking miles and miles (literally and figuratively) with me and speaking the truth into me. She was a constant reminder that I needed to take my eyes off circumstances and put them on the face of Jesus. I'm not sure how I would have made it had God not brought her into my life at that exact time. Donna often told me her words would mean nothing if I were not teachable and were not willing to have a heart to listen. I believe it is when we offer God our emptiness in complete humility and surrender that He, in turn, grants us incredible power to face our darkest hour. I often wonder what voice I'd have listened to if she had not been willing to enter my darkness or where I'd be had I not been willing to hear.

Looking back, it's easier now to see the many times God showed up. Sometimes, he used his people; often, it was acts of kindness somebody had shown, and other times, it was an unexpected gift. Donna was one of those gifts for me. There is nothing sweeter than looking back on this journey and seeing the beautiful handprints God left behind.

Lady At The Grave

After the funeral, I became obsessed with Heaven. I needed to know where my son was. I had sheltered him and cared for him for years. I had so many unanswered questions. Was he still eleven years old? Do they fish in Heaven? Does he know how much evil is in the world now? Can he see me crying for him? I needed answers and no longer wanted to be in this earthly body. I wanted to be with my son and join him in his new home. I was struggling, and Heaven was all I could think about.

My twin sister and I visited the cemetery daily. On one visit, we saw a little old lady visiting her husband's grave a few feet from where Paul Michael was buried. We began talking with her about her husband, who had passed away some time ago. This old lady pointed to Paul Michael's grave, which wasn't marked yet, and asked who it was for. I told her it was my eleven-year-old son who died suddenly a couple of weeks ago. She gasped in horror and said, "Oh my goodness!" I saw the concern on her face and said, "I'll be alright. God will give me strength to get through this." In a harsh, firm tone, the little old lady looked straight into my eyes and said, "Let me tell you something; you are right; God will give you the strength, but He AIN'T gonna do it for you. You must get up and do it yourself! Then He will give you the strength to do it!"

I looked at my sister, whose chin had just dropped. The look on her face reflected what I knew she was thinking. Did this old lady need to speak with such harshness in her voice to someone who is hurting so deeply? The truth is she did need to; this old lady, in her wisdom, had experienced her own grief, and she knew the grief of losing a child would be the hardest and deepest of all pain. Her words stung, but they sunk deep into my heart. She knew what lay ahead for me and could read the thoughts still raging inside me... *Oh, God, I don't think I can do this! I don't want to do this!* All I wanted was to go to Heaven to be with Paul Michael, where there was no more pain.

Don Piper once said that sometimes we are so heavenly bound we are no earthly good. Those words were fit for me. I wanted to leave this world. I wanted to die. I believe the words that lady spoke harshly to me that day were words God put on her heart to say to me because He knew I needed to hear them. The words spoke truth: God wouldn't do this *for* me, but He promised to do it *with* me.

I never saw that little old lady again, but I knew God had put her there for me that day. I wasn't sure how I was going to do it. How would I continue to do life when I no longer wanted to live? At about 2 a.m. the following day, I woke up and went downstairs

221

to the office. I picked up my Bible and read Isaiah 40:31, which says, "*Those who HOPE in the Lord will renew their strength. They will soar on wings like eagles; they will run and not grow weary, they will walk but will not faint.*" It was a reminder that God promised Paul Michael and I would someday be reunited together in Heaven for eternity. I had to make a decision, and this little lady recognized it. I could stand firm on God's promises and persevere, trusting him to be my strength and choose to live, or I could allow my pain to stop me from living and die to everything I had ever believed in. My decision to keep going wasn't an easy one. It meant choosing faith over despair. It meant getting up instead of giving up.

Waves

Grief is a funny thing. The waves accompanying grief are as sudden and unexpected as the day my son went to Heaven. Emotions were constantly changing and catching me off guard. One moment, I felt strong and somewhat in control, then, without warning, I'd find myself in a fetal position, gripped in agonizing pain. It would happen randomly and without warning. If I drove by the park where he loved to fish, walked by the Legos at Walmart, went to the church he attended with me, or did something as simple as seeing a blonde-haired boy walking down the street, I'd lose it; the floodgate of tears would reopen. I had never lost anyone close to me before, so I was completely unaware there were so-called stages of grief. I was convinced I was losing my mind.

I actually made an appointment with my doctor to be evaluated. Then, as God often did, he left another handprint. I went to the mailbox, and there was a package from Vicki D., one of my co-workers. She had no way of knowing what I was experiencing at the time, but the Lord had put it on her heart to send me an interview of two families who had lost all three children at one time. One of the fathers said, "Grief is like you are standing in the ocean-facing the shore, standing on two feet, when out of nowhere a wave hits you from behind and knocks you to your knees. The force is so strong you can't get up. That's what grief is like. You just never know when the waves will hit." His words stopped me in my tracks. I realized at that moment that I wasn't going crazy; I was grieving!

Stuck

There is a difference between grieving as a Christian and grieving without hope. Being a Christian doesn't mean we don't hurt. We hurt terribly! We cry loudly! We wrestle with the Lord as we grieve. But as we grieve, we hold tight to the anchor of our faith. But one thing is sure: everyone who walks through the valley of the shadow of death will ultimately have to make a choice—the choice to trust and surrender to His will or harbor anger, bitterness, and resentment. I have often wondered what choice I'd have made if it had happened eight years earlier when I wasn't walking with the Lord. I'm confident I would have blamed God, and I'm sure my confident hope of eternity would instead be a deep sense of hopelessness. I experienced this early in my grief when I visited with a mother in Virginia after the passing of her daughter. Her house was dark, and the shades were closed. I remember her tone when she said, "I am so angry at God; I'm just so angry!" She was still there, stuck, angry at God, refusing to move on. And it had been over 17 years.

Anger Turned to Purpose

Finding purpose in his death was something that kept me up at night. I needed a glimpse of why God would allow a little boy who declared to be his servant to die. The world was full of evil people, and clearly, the world needed more boys like Paul Michael. This question was an area I continued to wrestle with, praying and asking God to show me something, anything, to help me move through it. I recognize that most parents long to know—but never find out—any purpose of their child's death. There are some things we will not know this side of Heaven. That's why it's called faith. Hebrews 11:1 says, *"Now faith is confidence in what we hope for and assurance about what we do not see."* We don't always get to understand the mysteries of Heaven or see the plan here below. But we do know God is sovereign, and even though we can't see and don't understand it, we can trust His will for our lives. God was merciful in my prayers and left another handprint in a very unexpected situation.

We had not heard from our neighbors who lived a few houses down the street. They had a young son Paul Michael's age, and spent much time playing together. Mike, the father, had been Paul Michael's assistant coach in soccer for a few years. I realize people aren't sure what to say or do when there is a tragedy this deep, but friends I thought would be there for me weren't, and friends I didn't expect to be wouldn't let go. But it hurt when friends that I knew loved my son remained utterly silent. The Johnson family had certainly been silent. We knew they didn't go to church and suspected if they didn't believe in God, they might be struggling with how to tell Nicholas his little buddy died and then having to explain what happens after death. The truth was, I was hurt and didn't really care about the reason for not acknowledging his death; I just cared that they didn't. I wondered if they had even cared enough to attend his funeral. I reached for the guest register book out of the drawer and searched every page, looking for their signature. Their names were nowhere in the book. Feelings of hurt had now turned to anger.

One day, my sister and I walked our dogs to Green Valley Park, following our usual route. We began reminiscing about everything we had done with Paul Michael at that park. "How many hours do you think we spent sitting under that tree while Paul Michael fished?" I asked. "More than we can count sis," Vickie said. We walked by the soccer field where Paul Michael had played for years, and I could feel bitterness rearing its ugly head again. I reflected on the years Paul Michael played soccer with Mike as his assistant coach. As we turned the corner on the walking trail, I heard someone yell, "Connie!" I looked up and saw Jo Johnson standing at the end of the corner.

My heart started to race. What would I say? I suspected this moment would eventually come and wasn't sure how to respond. It would have seemed easy to ignore her like I thought she had done to me, but I couldn't. Jo was holding out her hands to hug me as I approached her. I embraced her and asked if we could take a walk. She politely agreed. I asked Vickie to take the dogs home while Jo and I visited.

We began making small talk, and then I decided to bite the bullet and ask what had been heavy on my heart. I stated, "Jo, I have not heard one word from you since Paul Michael died. You haven't acknowledged his life or his death." With a look of regret, she said, "Connie, I'm so sorry. I have a soccer ball that all the kids signed, and I've wanted to bring it by, but I just haven't been able to yet." She continued, "When I was younger, my brother died, and I was devastated. It was very painful for me, and I just haven't been able to do it. We love Paul Michael, Connie!"

"I know you do," I said, "and that's why it's been so hard for me to understand. You guys didn't even attend his funeral."

She replied, "No, I didn't, but Mike and Nicholas went."

I started feeling like a heel but said, "I checked the registration book, and their names weren't in it."

She responded, "Connie, you know Mike well enough to know he isn't going to stand in a long line to sign a book."

She continued, "Paul Michael's death has really affected Nicholas. Nicholas has Paul Michael's picture as his wallpaper and hung his funeral bulletin on his bedroom wall. He even wrote Paul Michael's name all over his notebooks. A while back, Nicholas came to me and said, 'Mom, I want to know Jesus the way Paul Michael knew Jesus.' I said, 'Okay, Nicholas,' and left it at that. But he came back a few days later and said, 'Mom, I really want to know Jesus the way Paul Michael knew Jesus.' So I asked him, 'What do you want? Do you want to go to church?' He said, 'Yes, Mom, I do.'"

She went on, "Connie, we all started going to church and have been attending ever since. We all love it!"

My heart began to race. Clearly, I had misjudged this precious family. I couldn't hold back the tears any longer and said, "Jo, I need to go. Thank you for sharing that with me."

I hugged her tight and started walking home. I couldn't stop the tears and began repenting for my unforgiving heart. God had been working behind the scenes, building His Kingdom. Later, I heard more stories of how parents were parenting differently and more people who had turned their lives over to Christ after attending my son's funeral. One lady told me that in eleven years, Paul Michael produced more fruit for the Kingdom of Heaven than some do in a lifetime. I'm not going to say all this makes his death easier to bear, but it did help me realize there is a much bigger picture and plan than my eyes can see!

The Sketch

This was the day I had procrastinated long enough. It was time to clean out my son's things. I had prepared my mind for how painful this day would be, but preparing my heart was another story. Friends and family had offered to help, but I needed to be alone. Going through Paul Michael's things was sacred to me. It was a place only someone who lost a loved one could fully understand.

"Am I truly doing this?" I said to myself, shaking my head, "Is this even possible? Where do I begin?" The feelings and thoughts were almost overwhelming. I decided to start in the closet. One by one, I took his clothes off the hangers. His Fort Worth Christian uniforms were in front, then his basketball jerseys, then his purple TCU tee-shirt. Oh, he loved that T-shirt, I thought to myself. I recalled the TCU jersey that used to hang there, which Paul Michael was buried in. I looked down and saw dirty clothes on the floor at the closet's bottom. They still had "him" on them: the smell, the dirt, and the old sweat were still there. My heart couldn't take it anymore. I sat down sobbing uncontrollably, "Paul Michael!" I cried, screaming his name, "I'm sorry, I'm so sorry!" I wasn't sorry for something I did but because I couldn't save him. Lord knows I tried, but my attempt at CPR had not been successful; I felt like I had failed him.

I wanted to stop the cleaning out, but I knew if I did, I would find myself back there another day, having to finish the job. I decided to push and plow through. Next on the list were his toys. TCU and OU basketballs, baseballs, and footballs, the TCU bobbing horned frog he got at his first game. So many toys and gadgets, each holding precious memories that were a part of him. There were hundreds of Legos he had collected over the years. Legos were his second love, followed by fishing. I picked up the extra-large Lego race car on his shelf, remembering how astonished I was that he had put it together all by himself. It was hard to believe it was four months ago; it seemed like only yesterday.

I looked under his bed, surprised at how many things an eleven-year-old could stuff underneath it. I pulled out his sketchbook.

Flipping through the pages, I saw drawings of animals, gangsters, and many stick people fishing. Then I turned the page and gasped at what I saw next. In his own personal time and room, he had sketched a picture of Jesus. It was precious! Jesus was hanging on the cross with thorns on his head and crooked shoulders. It had his signature three crosses that he put on many of his personal things. What was Paul Michael thinking as he drew this sweet picture of Jesus, I asked myself. I sat there speechless at first. Then, tears of joy started to fall as I thanked God for another confirmation of where my little boy was at this very moment. I tore the sketch out of his book and put it away, wondering what I would do with this little treasure I found.

I shared what I had found with the ladies in my Bible Study Fellowship (BSF) leaders circle. Mindy approached me as we walked out and said, "Connie, you should make a Christmas card from Paul Michael's sketch." "Wow," I said, "What a great idea. I'll think about it." In my heart, I believed this sketch could somehow honor God. I laid it on top of my bed and knelt in prayer. I asked God to show me how to use this incredible piece of art to bring glory to His Son, not mine.

I discussed the idea of turning this sketch into a Christmas card with my friend Kathy. She said, "There is a print shop on Rufe Snow Drive that does custom printing. You should ask them if they could make a Christmas card out of it."

We drove to the print shop, and found the owner, whose name was John Paul. I found this interesting since people often confuse that name with Paul Michael. I introduced myself and shared the story behind the sketch. Looking around, I noticed pictures of his family on the walls, so I could tell he must be a family man.

John Paul was incredibly kind and compassionate. He asked, "Was the story of your son's death on the news?"

"Yes," I replied. "It was."

"I saw that story," he said. "It was heartbreaking." Then he added, "I think we can darken the sketch and turn it into a Christmas card."

"That sounds great!" I said. "How much do you think it will cost?"

He asked, "How many do you want printed?"

"I'm not sure," I said. How about 500?

He replied, "It would probably cost around $1.00 each, not including the envelopes or the design."

Since finances were tight, I said, "Well, let's make it 300."

John Paul responded, "I'd like to design the cover for you at no charge."

I hugged him and said, "Thank you so much; that's very kind of you."

Three men walked in, saw the embrace, and began teasing John Paul. It was clear they were regulars. "Hey," they jokingly said, "If we give you a hug, will you give us a discount?"

We all laughed. The men had no idea about the heartfelt conversation that had just taken place.

After leaving the print shop, Vickie and I went to Walmart to run some errands. Just as I was about to exit the car, my phone rang. It was John Paul. He said, "Connie, I hope it's okay, but I shared your story with the three men who walked in just as you left. One of them is a successful businessman who wishes to remain anonymous but wants to purchase all 500 of your Christmas cards." I was so surprised that I almost dropped the phone. I said, "I don't know what to say!" John Paul replied, "He wants to do this for you." I asked, "Can I get his address so I can send him a thank-you card?" John Paul explained, "No, he really wants to stay anonymous." He said, "All I need from you are the words you want printed on the card so we can get started."

My prayer had been that this sketch would somehow be a blessing, and God had just confirmed it! Later, I discovered that I had gone to the wrong print shop; it wasn't the one Kathy had sent me to but rather the one God had intended for me.

I mailed out hundreds of Christmas cards, and the response was overwhelming. A card must have hung on every refrigerator in the metroplex. I received one confirmation after another of people writing to tell me the Christmas card had changed the way they parent, helped them never take one day for granted, and reminded them of what HOPE is. I have no doubt Paul Michael would be pleased knowing this sketch had brought so much glory to his precious Jesus!

The Terrible "Firsts"

The "firsts" were the worst. His first birthday, the first anniversary of his heaven date, and all holidays suddenly changed from days filled with joy to days so hard they became almost unbearable. I recall the first Christmas season, I was at Hobby Lobby standing dumbfounded in the floral section. All I could think about was how other parents were shopping for their children's Christmas gifts while I was shopping for Christmas flowers for my son's grave. It was surreal and heartbreaking. Everyone else's lives kept moving forward, but my life stopped. I understood it because those parents still had their kids to live for, but my son was gone from this world. I couldn't have hidden the tears if I wanted to, so, as I continued shopping for the perfect Christmas flowers, I succumbed to the tears and allowed them to flow freely.

Mother's Day weekend was notoriously the hardest of all. Every year, that same weekend would roll around, reminding me of what used to be. It was the weekend I continually wanted to disappear. Once again, beginning with the first year after his death, the Lord used one of His best women to come to my aid, leaving another solid handprint of His faithfulness. Lauri was Addison's mother, another school friend of Paul Michael's. Lauri was the kindest person I had ever met, and her generosity was as big as her heart. She knew Mother's Day was fast approaching, and she was aware of the pain that accompanied it. Lauri asked me if I would like to get away and go to Vail, Colorado, for my first Mother's Day without Paul Michael.

Lauri had points at the Hyatt, which had a workout facility, a full kitchen, an outside hot tub, and an incredible view of the snow-covered mountain. She even offered a two-bedroom so my sister and her husband could join us. I can't adequately describe her kindness and the blessing it brought to me. It was exactly what I needed! Lauri didn't stop there; she had arranged for all the children in Paul Michael's class to write me a letter or card about him. She tied it in a beautiful bow; they blessed my socks off! Lauri is the one who showed me how to comfort and love others who are hurting. She was so generous that for the next five years, Lauri continued to bless me and give me a respite in the mountains of Colorado.

Trusting God Takes Courage

Gladys, a precious African American lady in my BSF leader circle, commented to me one morning regarding Paul Michael's death. She said, "Connie, God has given you an opportunity. He doesn't give this opportunity to everyone, but he gave it to you, so, use it and don't waste it." I loved her tender heart and couldn't be offended because I knew she believed the words she spoke, and scripture confirmed them. It's hard to see how God can use something so awful and so tragic for good in any way. But God doesn't allow suffering in our lives to give Satan a foothold. Satan is the father of lies, and he comes to kill, steal, and destroy. Satan wants us to remain stuck in our pain, living our lives out in misery and bitterness. But God wants better. He sent Jesus to stop the destruction that Satan causes, encouraging us to live each day in hope and with a focus on eternity. Surrendering all the pain to Jesus isn't easy. Trusting God takes courage. Romans 8:18 tells us that our sufferings are not worth comparing with the glory that will be revealed to us.

So, what do we do in the interim while we wait? James 1:12 reminds us, *"Blessed is the man who remains steadfast under trial, for when he has stood the test, he will receive the crown of life, which God has promised to those who love him."* God has made it clear that we still have purpose in our time of waiting, and that purpose is to run the race set before us! 2 Timothy 4:7-8 says, *"I have fought the good fight, I have finished the race, I have kept the faith."*

Not Wasted

Lauri's generosity in a respite created a desire in me to help other parents who have lost a child. The time spent reading God's word in those beautiful mountains of Colorado was deeply impactful. I began having an intense longing to come alongside other parents who have also lost a child. Second Corinthians 1:4 encourages us that God comforts us in all our troubles so that we can comfort those in any trouble with the comfort we ourselves receive from God. It had become clear to me what Gladys said regarding my sufferings being an opportunity. I chose to trust her advice on not wasting it.

I can't do anything to bring my son back, but I can do something here on earth with the time I have left. The Bible tells us we all have gifts and should use them for God's glory. Empathy and compassion have become my strongest gifts. My family and I decided to start a 501(c)3 to help assist families in whatever ways we can after the loss of a child. We have sent many families on respites, helped some with finances, and told the beautiful story of

Jesus to many hurting hearts. Each person in this book has chosen daily surrender in view of an eternal perspective. It's true; it takes courage to trust God and requires us to surrender to a faithful God. I believe surrender is such an important form of worship, that I named our nonprofit *Eternal Surrender*.

I want to speak to you from the deepest part of my heart as a mother who has walked through the unimaginable pain of losing a child. Grief is a journey that feels unbearable at times, and I know firsthand how consuming it can be. In those moments of darkness, it can be hard to believe that anything good could come from such pain. But I've learned something that I want to share with you: God is faithful, and He will be glorified through your pain.

In Scripture, we see so many who suffered deeply, yet their faith in God held strong. Paul, struggling with his own deep anguish, asked God to take away his suffering. And God's response was clear: "My grace is sufficient for you, for my power is made perfect in weakness" (2 Corinthians 12:9). One of my favorites, Job, endured immense suffering. He lost everything, yet he never turned away from God. He never received an answer to the "why" of his pain. Instead, God revealed to Job a deeper understanding of who He is and His sovereignty. Job was always a man of faith, but through his suffering, his faith grew stronger, and he gained a much clearer vision of the God he worshiped.

David, though burdened by the consequences of his own actions, never lost his trust in God's plan. And Joseph, wrongfully imprisoned and betrayed by those closest to him, remained faithful. These stories remind us that in the hardest times, God's sovereignty remains. He uses our suffering to shape us for His glory.

When my grief was at its most overwhelming, there were moments when I couldn't see God. But looking back, I now see

His handprint in every step I took. Even in the darkest places, He was there, guiding me in ways I didn't understand at the time. I know now that even when you don't feel His presence, God is still working. You can trust Him in complete surrender, even when the road ahead seems impossible. I know how hard it is to believe these truths when your heart feels shattered, when the weight of grief is suffocating. But I've walked this path, and I can tell you this with all certainty: as you choose to surrender your pain to Him, God is faithful.

There is a sacred beauty in surrender—the kind that blooms when our deepest pain is placed into the hand of the One who never lets go. The love you carry for your child is eternal, the ache may never fully leave, but in Christ we have eternal life. His promises are true; through Him we will be reunited in eternity. As you lay every tear, every question, and every longing before Him, may you find peace that surpasses all understanding and the quiet strength to live each day in eternal surrender.

You are not alone. He is with you, and I promise, you can trust Him. Trust that He will use your pain for His glory. Trust that He is working in ways you can't see yet. He is trustworthy and faithful. Always.

I promise, you can trust Him.

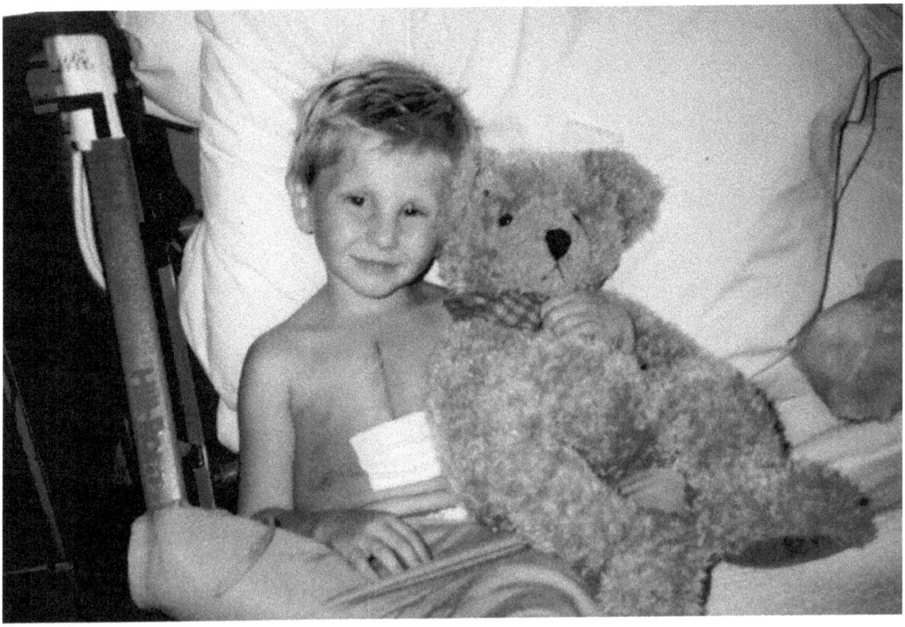

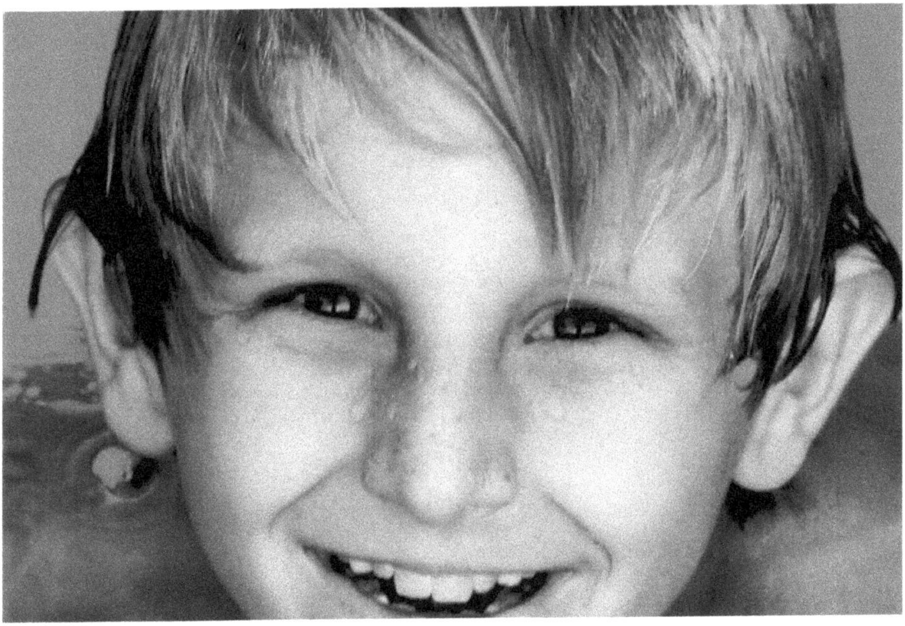

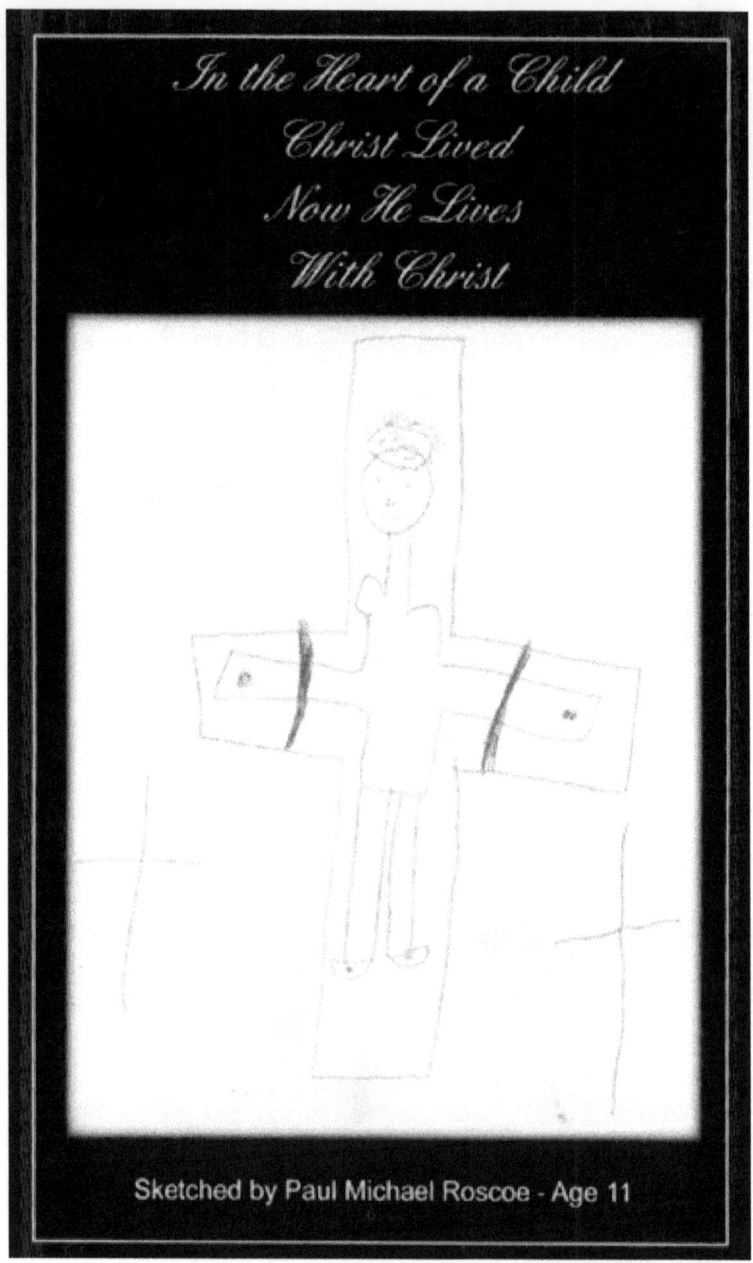

In the Heart of a Child
Christ Lived
Now He Lives
With Christ

Sketched by Paul Michael Roscoe - Age 11

www.ingramcontent.com/pod-product-compliance
Lightning Source LLC
Chambersburg PA
CBHW051511120626
46551CB00012B/875